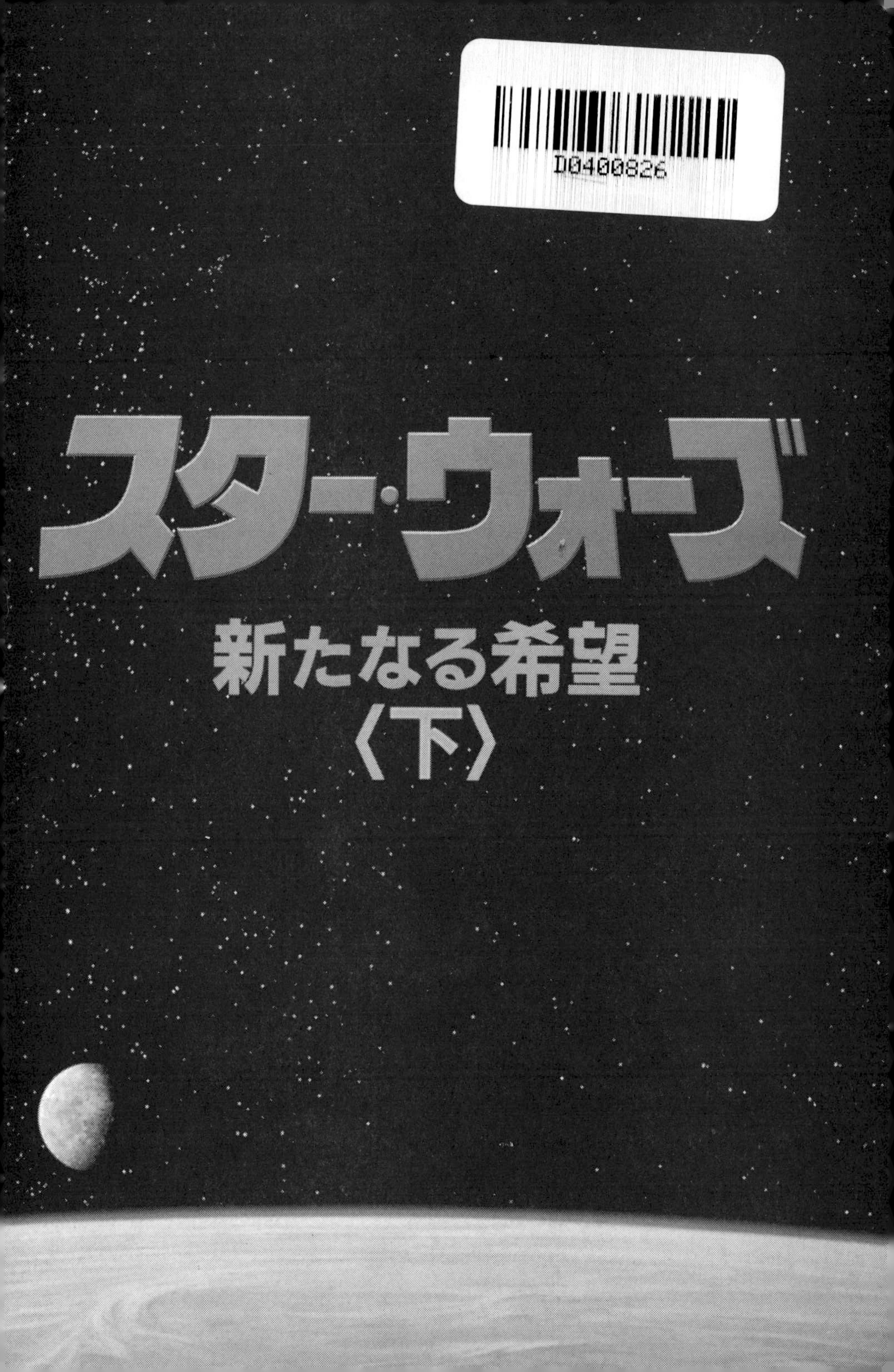
スター・ウォーズ
新たなる希望
〈下〉

"WHERE DO YOU THINK YOU'RE GOING?"

STAR WARS: A NEW HOPE — MANGA is a translation which was first published in Japan by Media Works. In Japan, manga is normally read from right-to-left. In order to conform to Western standards, the art in this book was copied in a mirror-image to facilitate left-to-right reading of the pages. This, of course, can cause some confusion in a story such as STAR WARS: A NEW HOPE — MANGA where readers are somewhat familiar with the material and so will notice characters both moving and appearing in an opposite fashion from that which they did in the film. We apologize for any confusion this may cause and hope that it will not detract from your enjoyment of this volume.

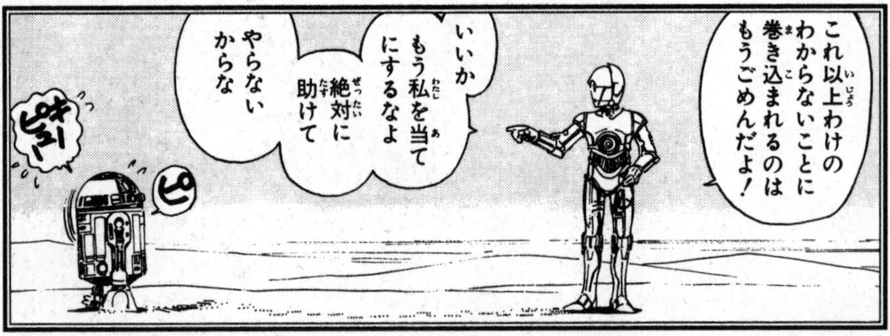
これ以上わけのわからないことに巻き込まれるのはもうごめんだよ！
いいか もう私を当てにするなよ 絶対に助けて
やらないからな
ピ
ピキュー

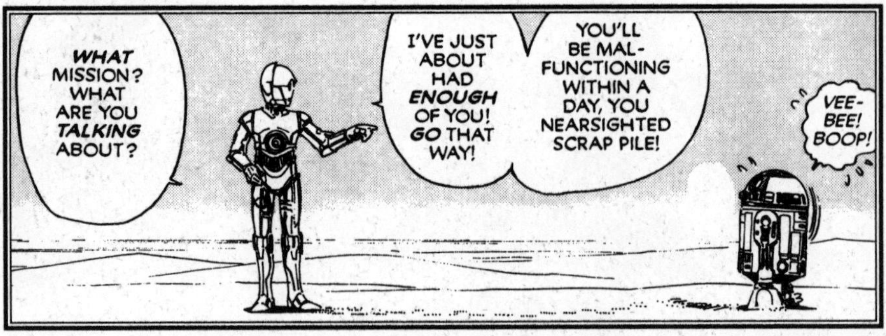
WHAT MISSION? WHAT ARE YOU TALKING ABOUT?
I'VE JUST ABOUT HAD ENOUGH OF YOU! GO THAT WAY!
YOU'LL BE MAL-FUNCTIONING WITHIN A DAY, YOU NEARSIGHTED SCRAP PILE!
VEE-BEE! BOOP!

A long time ago in a galaxy far, far away....

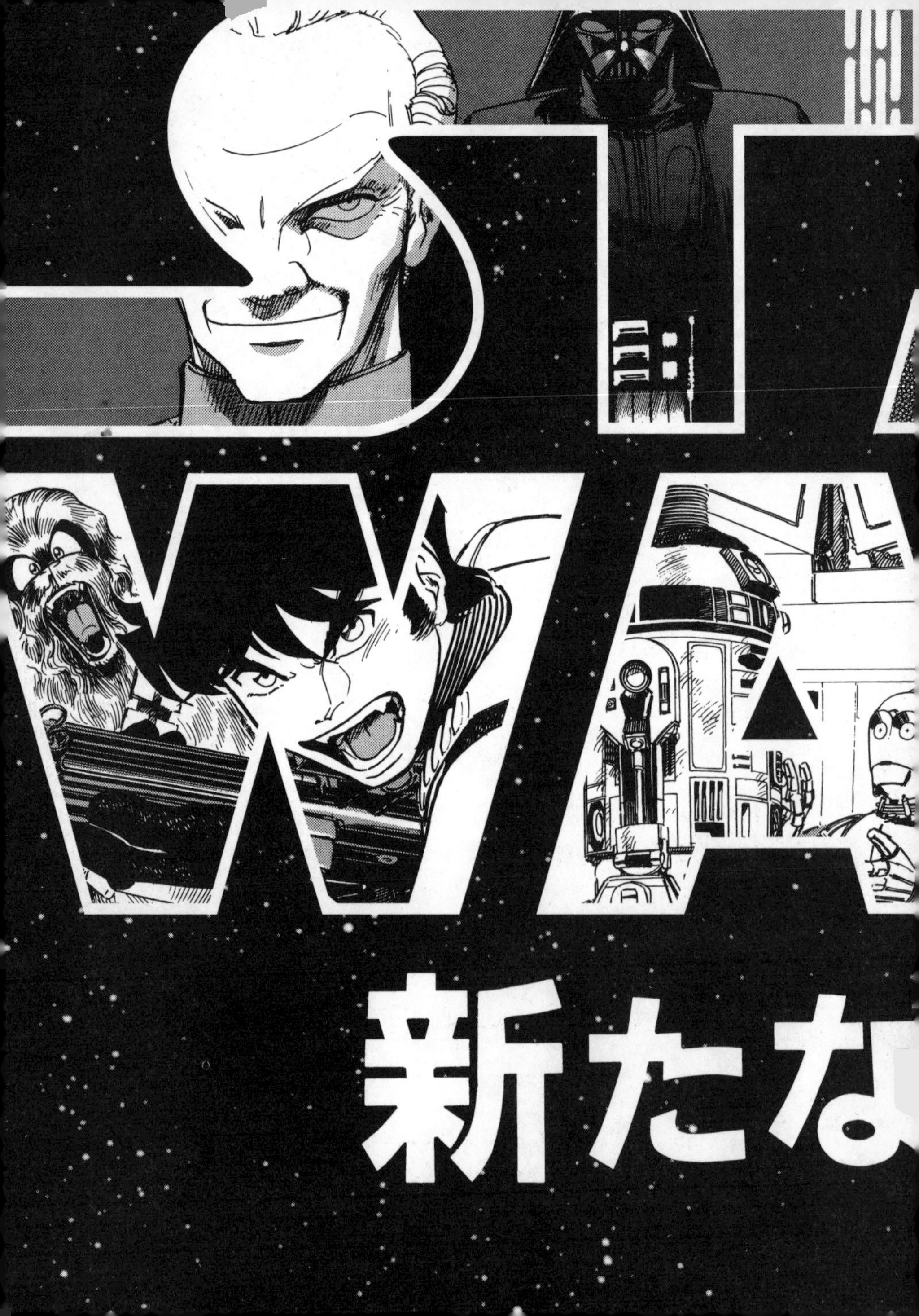
新たな

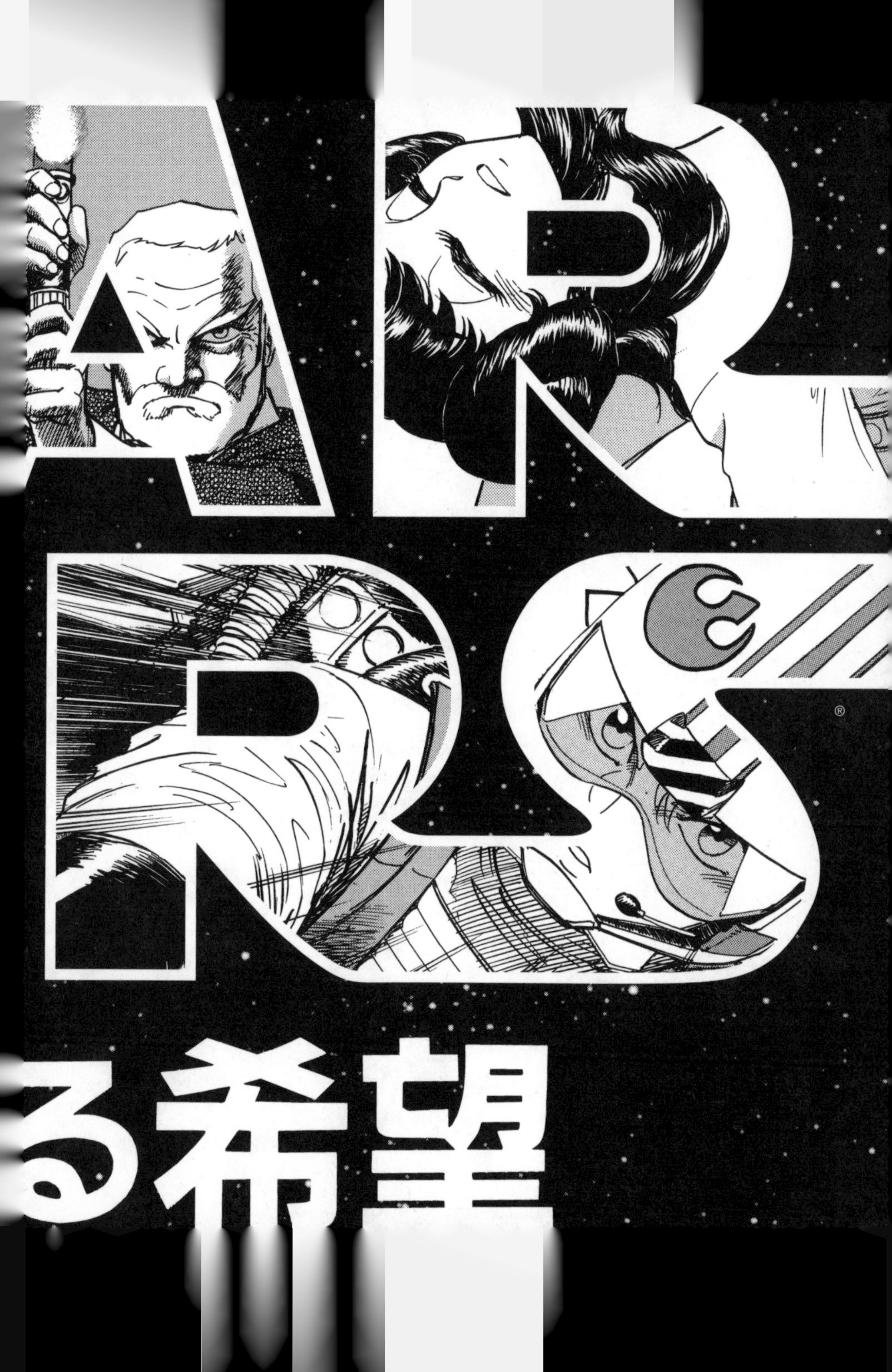
る希望

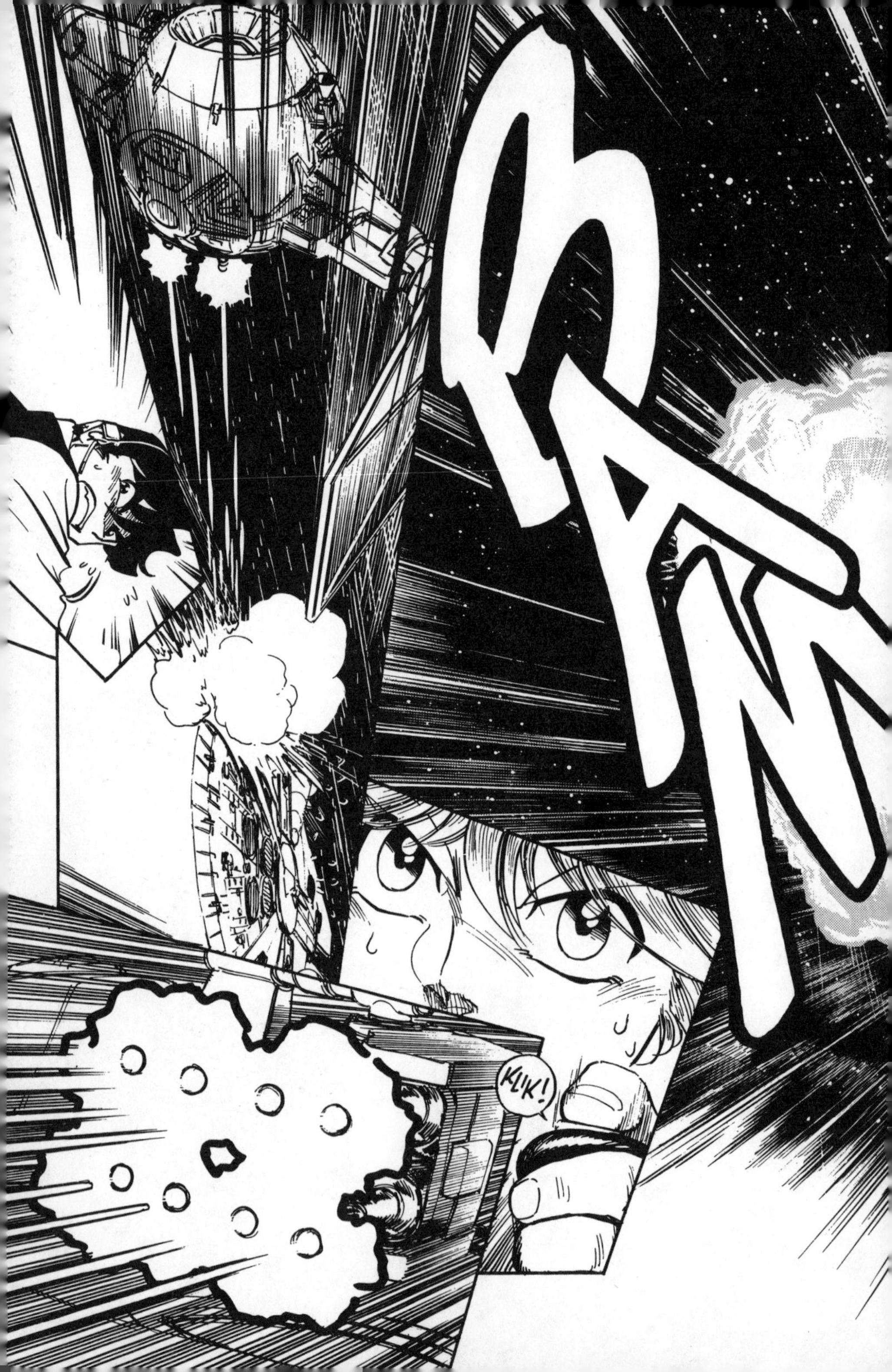
BAM
KLIK!

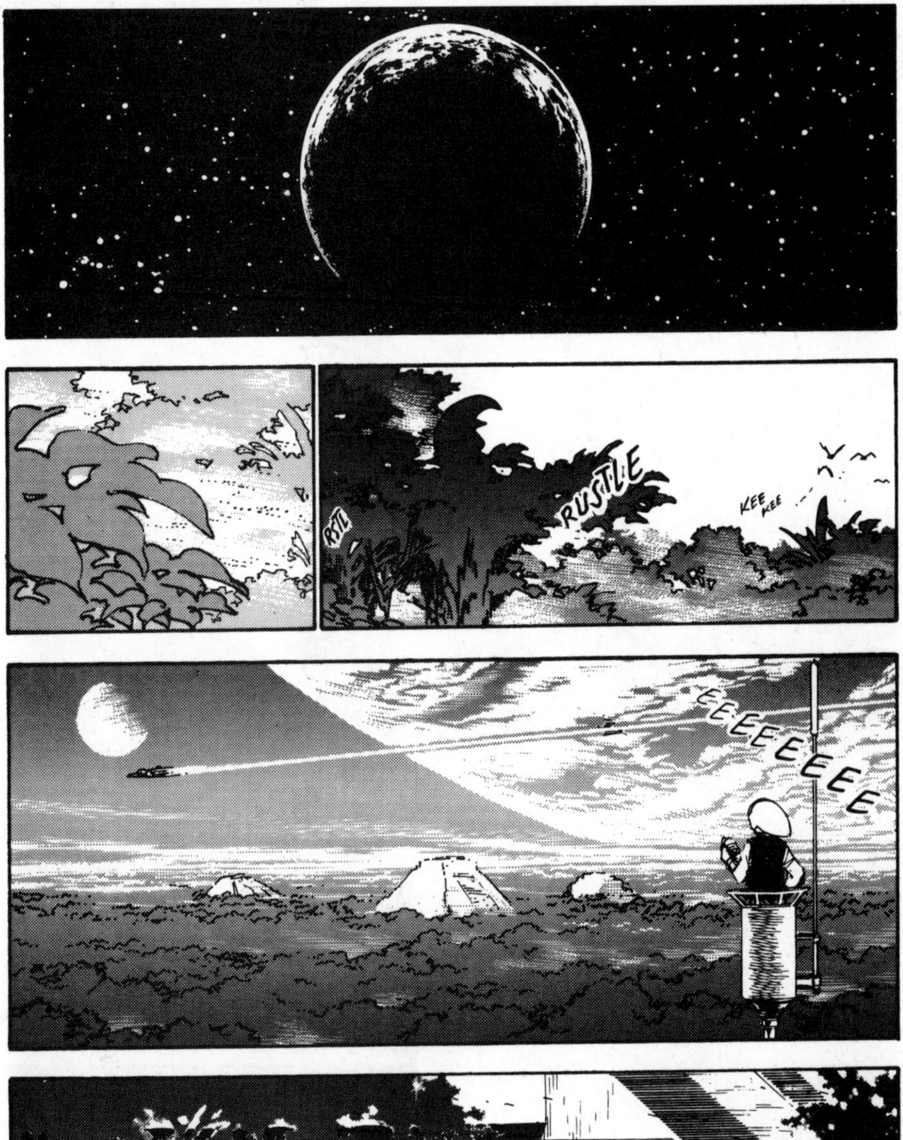
RSTL
RUSTLE
KEE KEE
EEEEEEEE

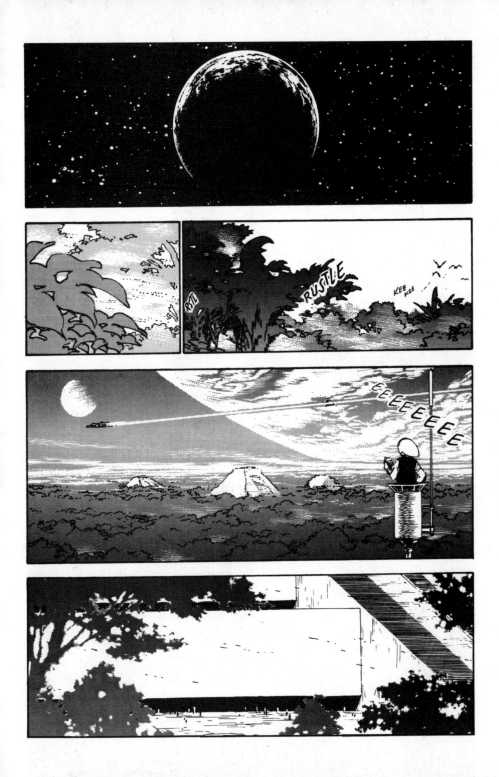

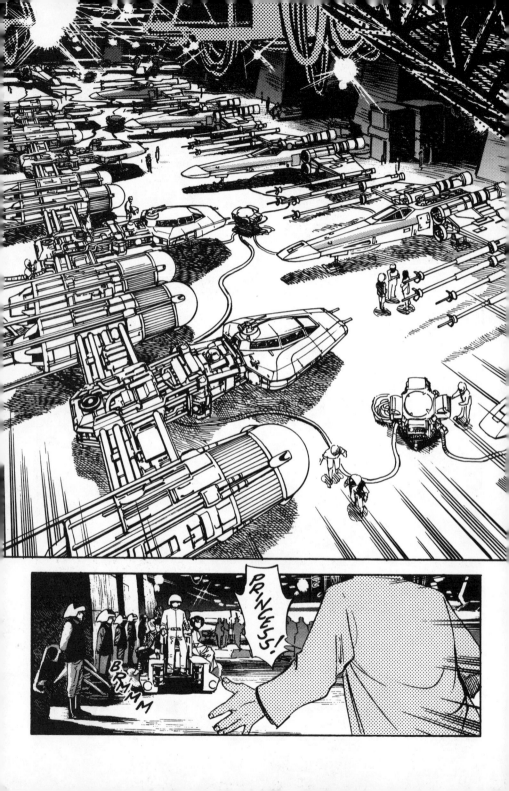

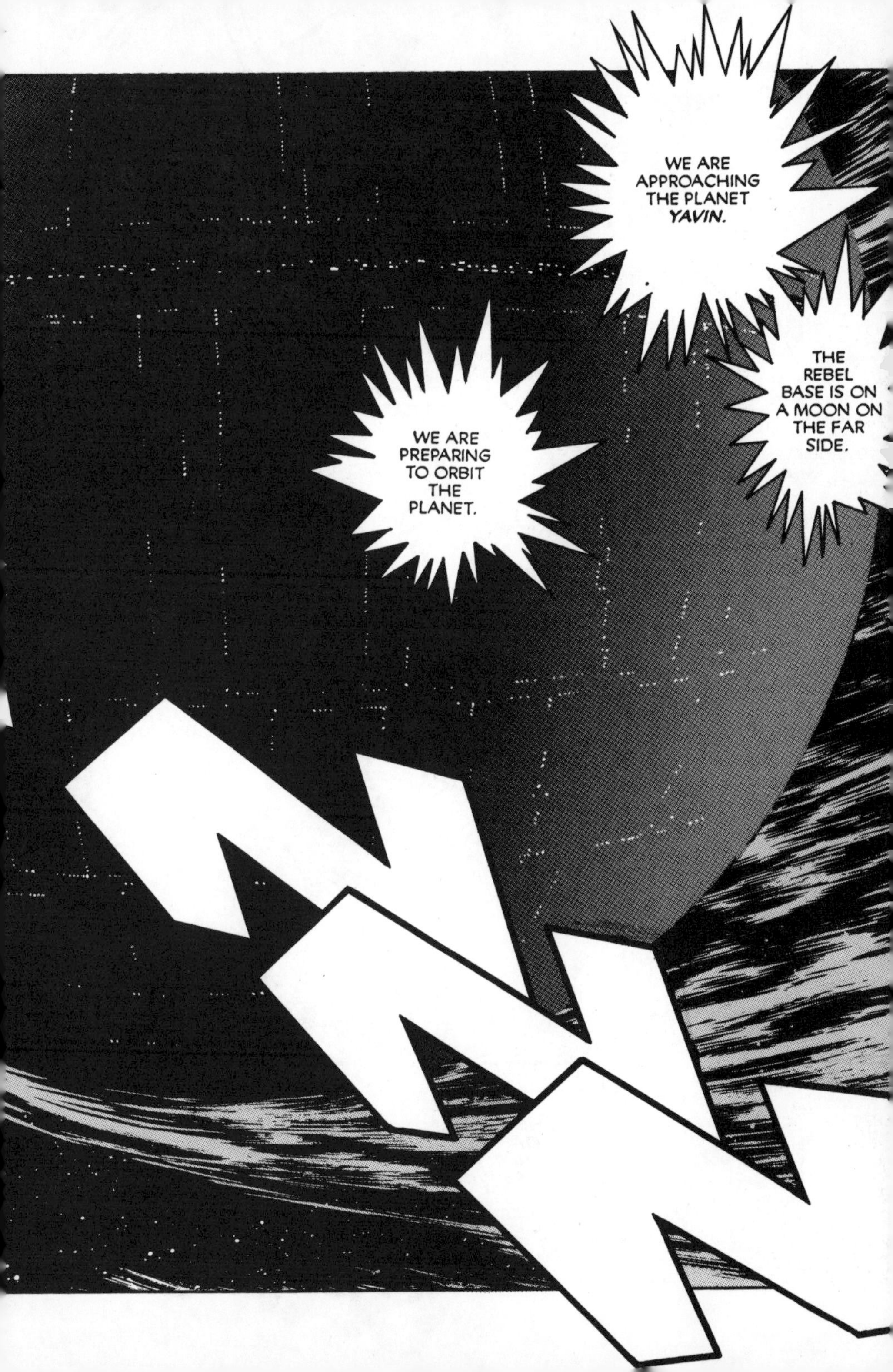
WE ARE APPROACHING THE PLANET *YAVIN.*
THE REBEL BASE IS ON A MOON ON THE FAR SIDE.
WE ARE PREPARING TO ORBIT THE PLANET.

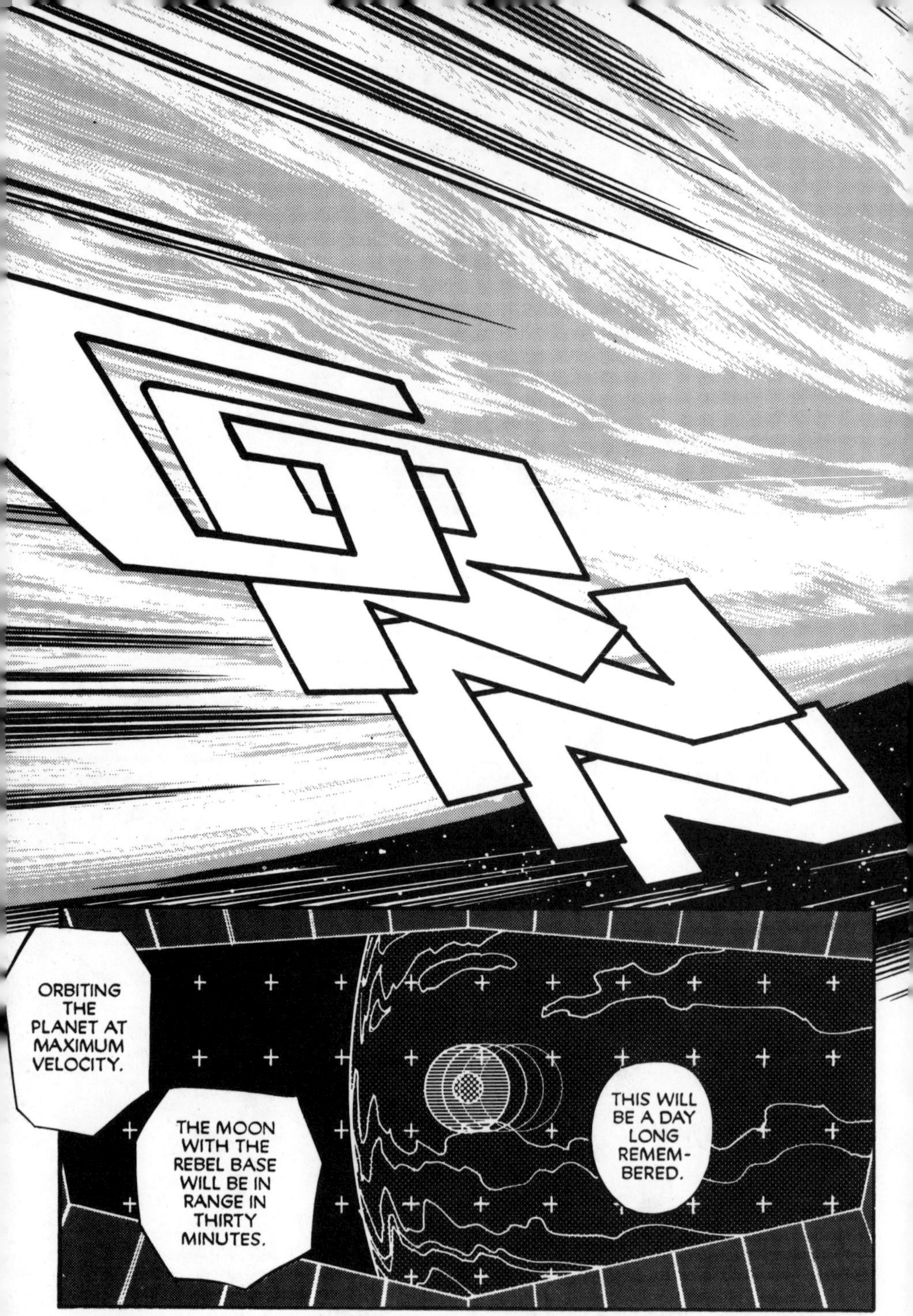
ORBITING THE PLANET AT MAXIMUM VELOCITY.
THE MOON WITH THE REBEL BASE WILL BE IN RANGE IN THIRTY MINUTES.
THIS WILL BE A DAY LONG REMEMBERED.

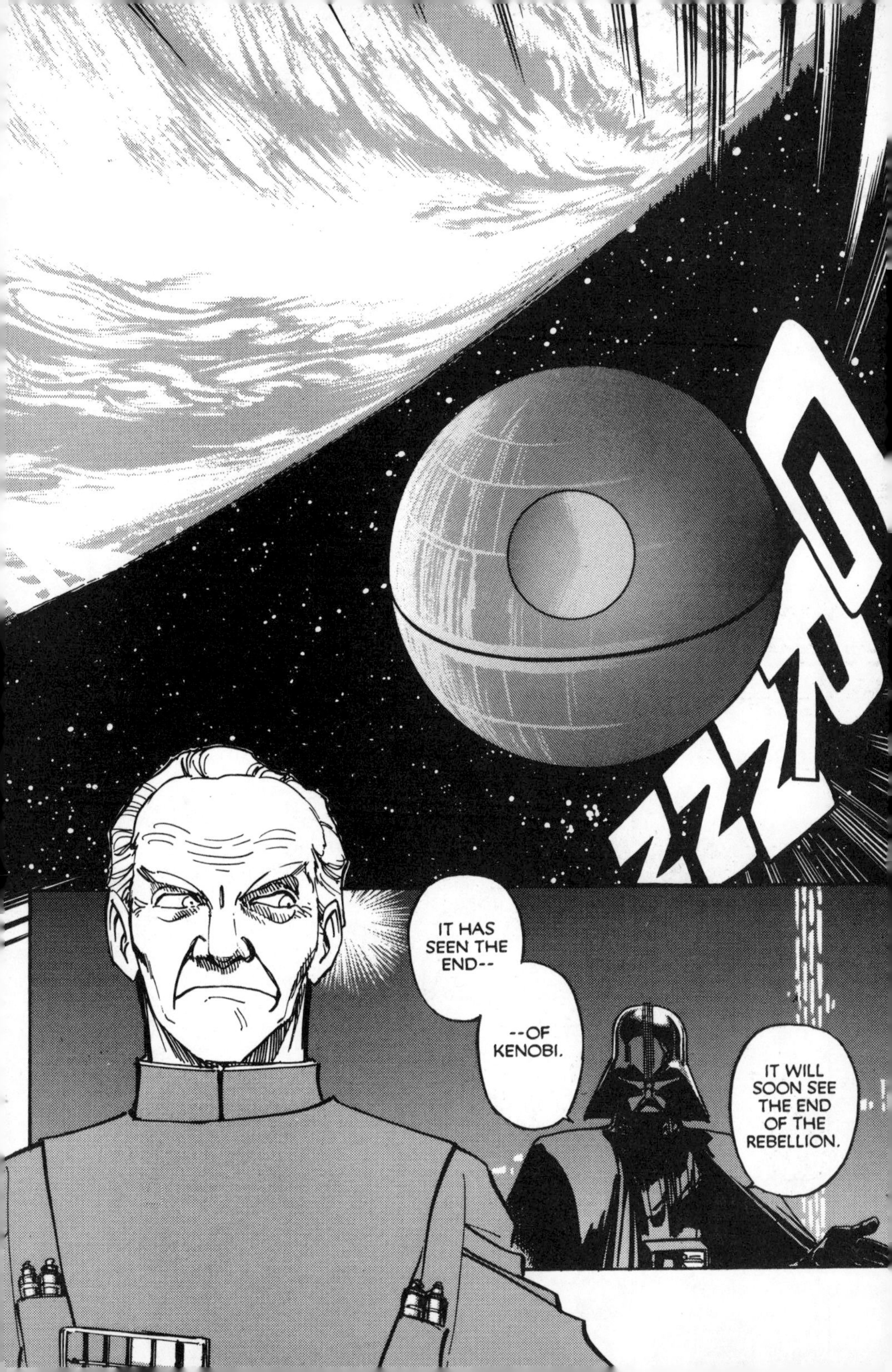
IT HAS SEEN THE END--
--OF KENOBI.
IT WILL SOON SEE THE END OF THE REBELLION.

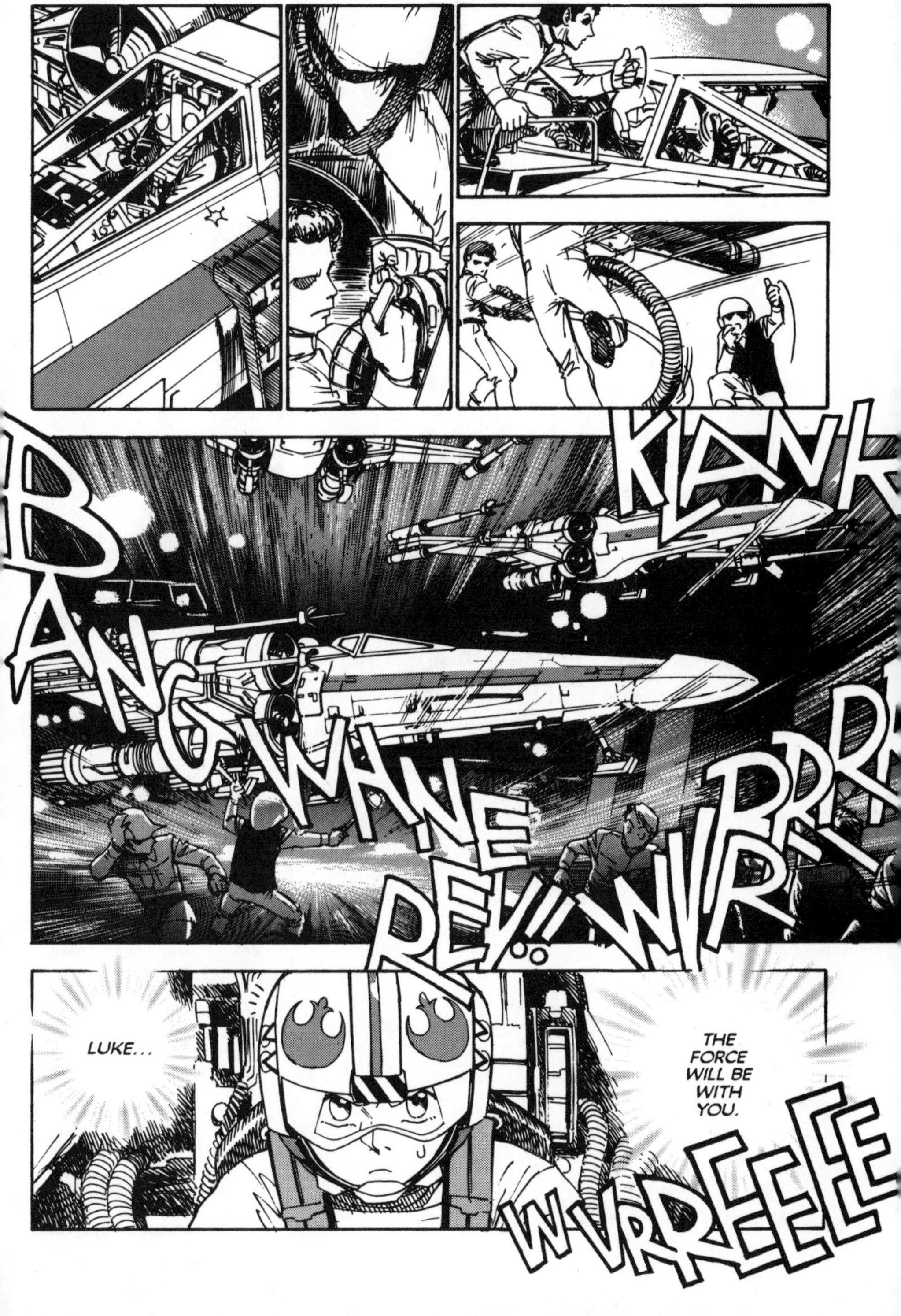
KLANK
BANG
LUKE...
THE FORCE WILL BE WITH YOU.

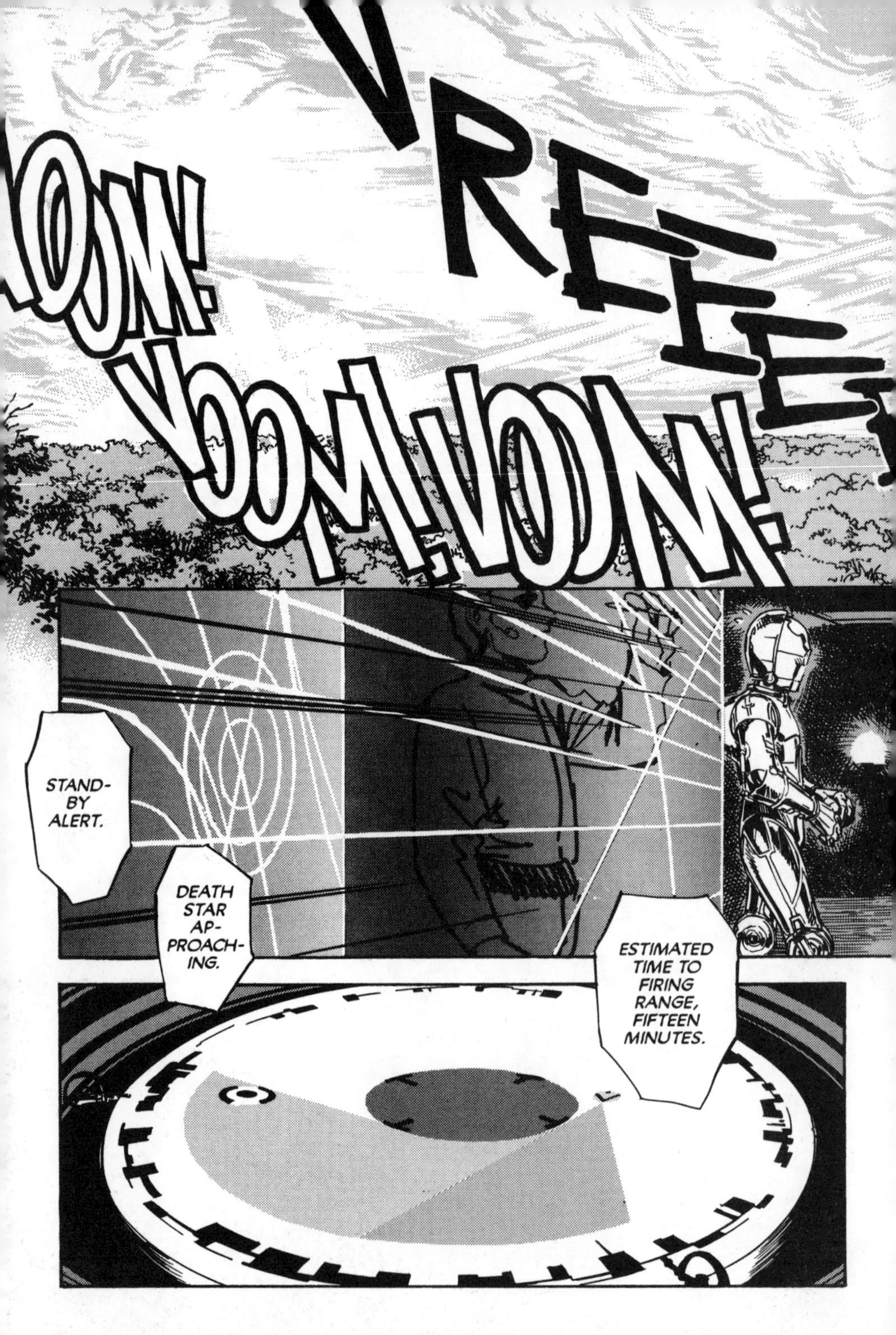

OOM!
VREEEE
VOOM! VOOM!
STAND-BY ALERT.
DEATH STAR AP-PROACH-ING.
ESTIMATED TIME TO FIRING RANGE, FIFTEEN MINUTES.

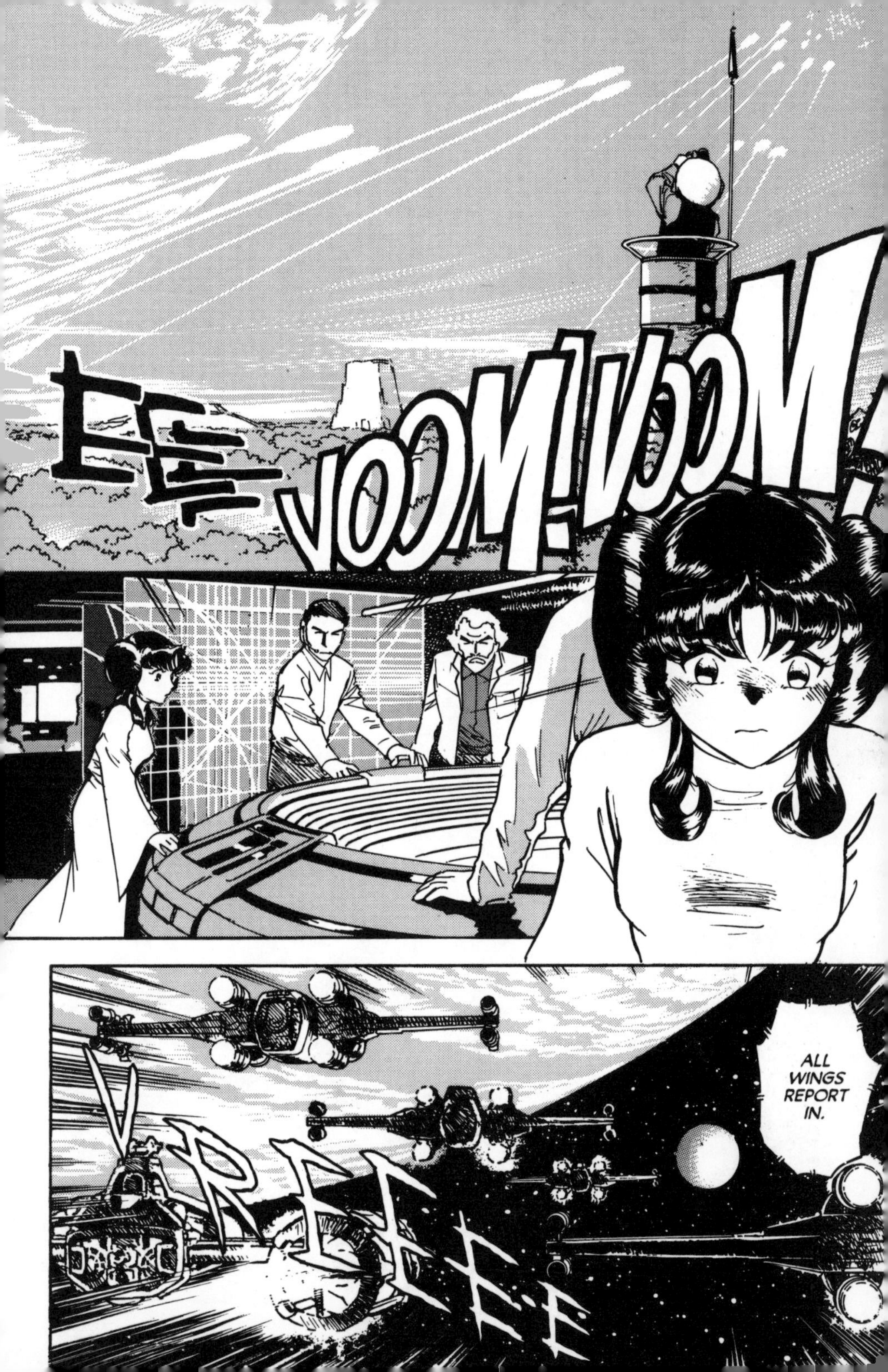
EEE
VOOM! VOOM!
VREEEE
ALL WINGS REPORT IN.

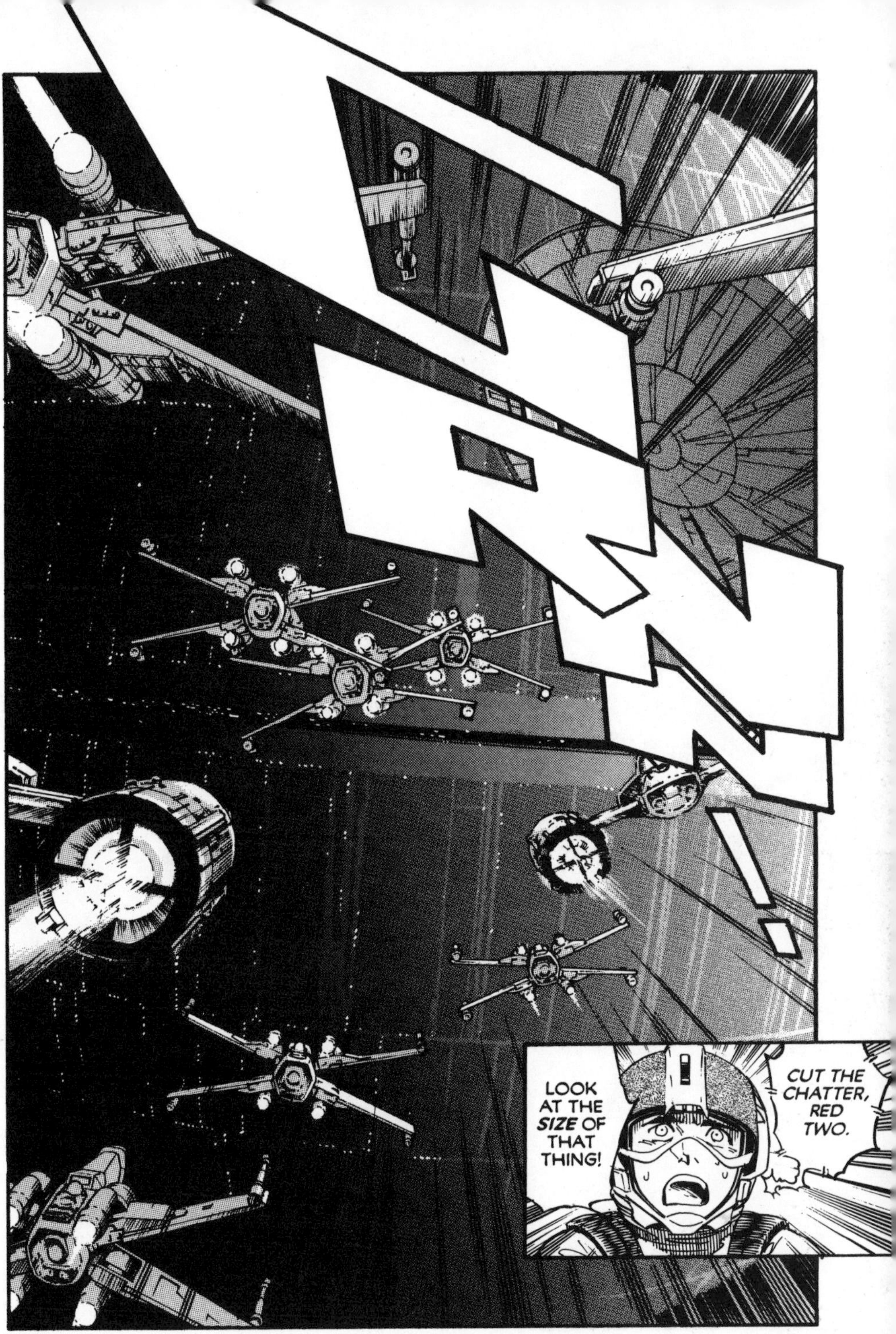
LOOK AT THE *SIZE* OF THAT THING!
CUT THE CHATTER, RED TWO.

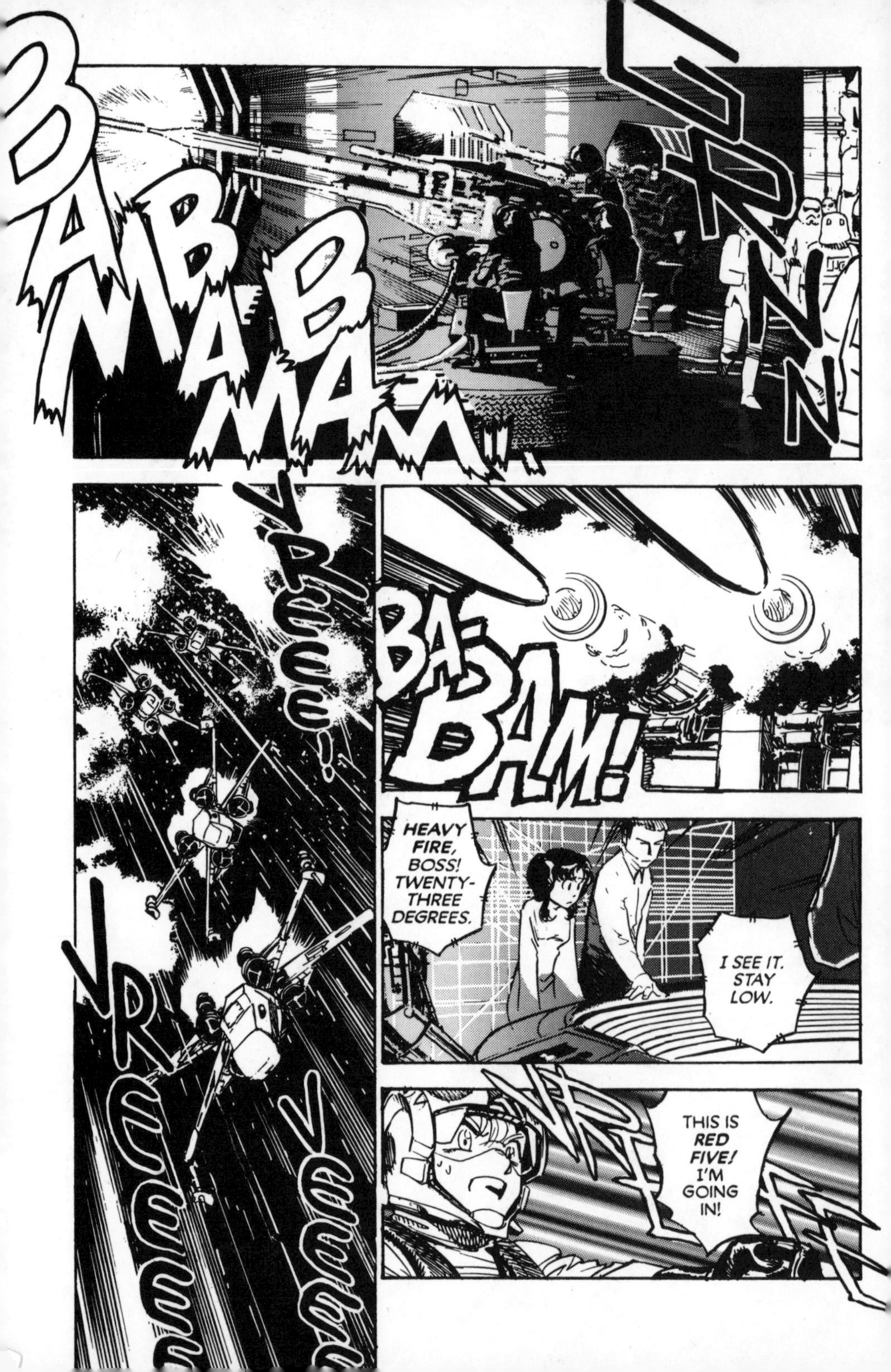
BAMBAMBAM!!!
VREEEE!
BA-BAM!
HEAVY FIRE, BOSS! TWENTY-THREE DEGREES.
I SEE IT. STAY LOW.
THIS IS RED FIVE! I'M GOING IN!

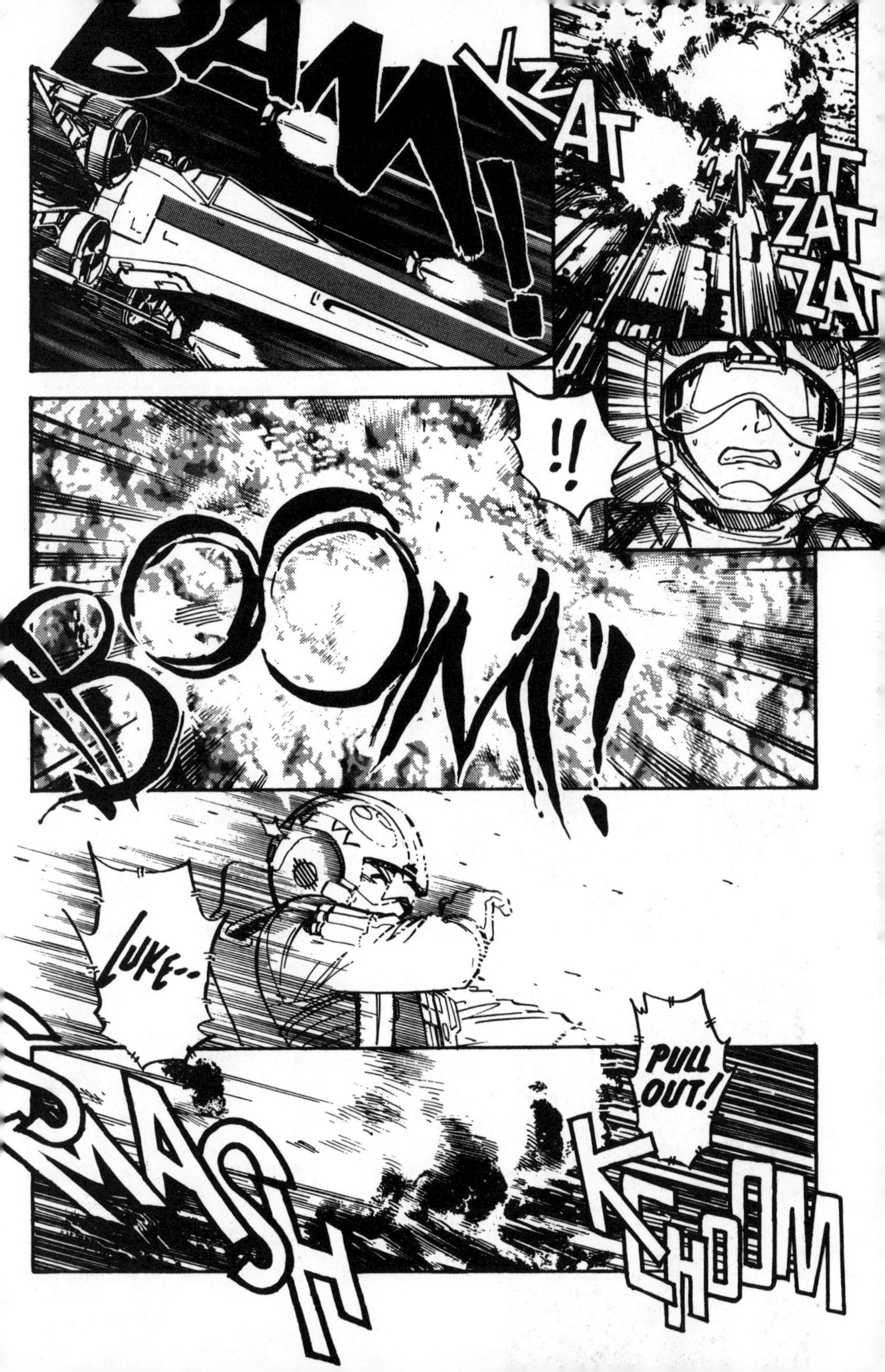
BAM!
ZZAT
ZAT ZAT ZAT ZAT
!!
BOOM!
LUKE--
PULL OUT!
SMASH
KCHOOM

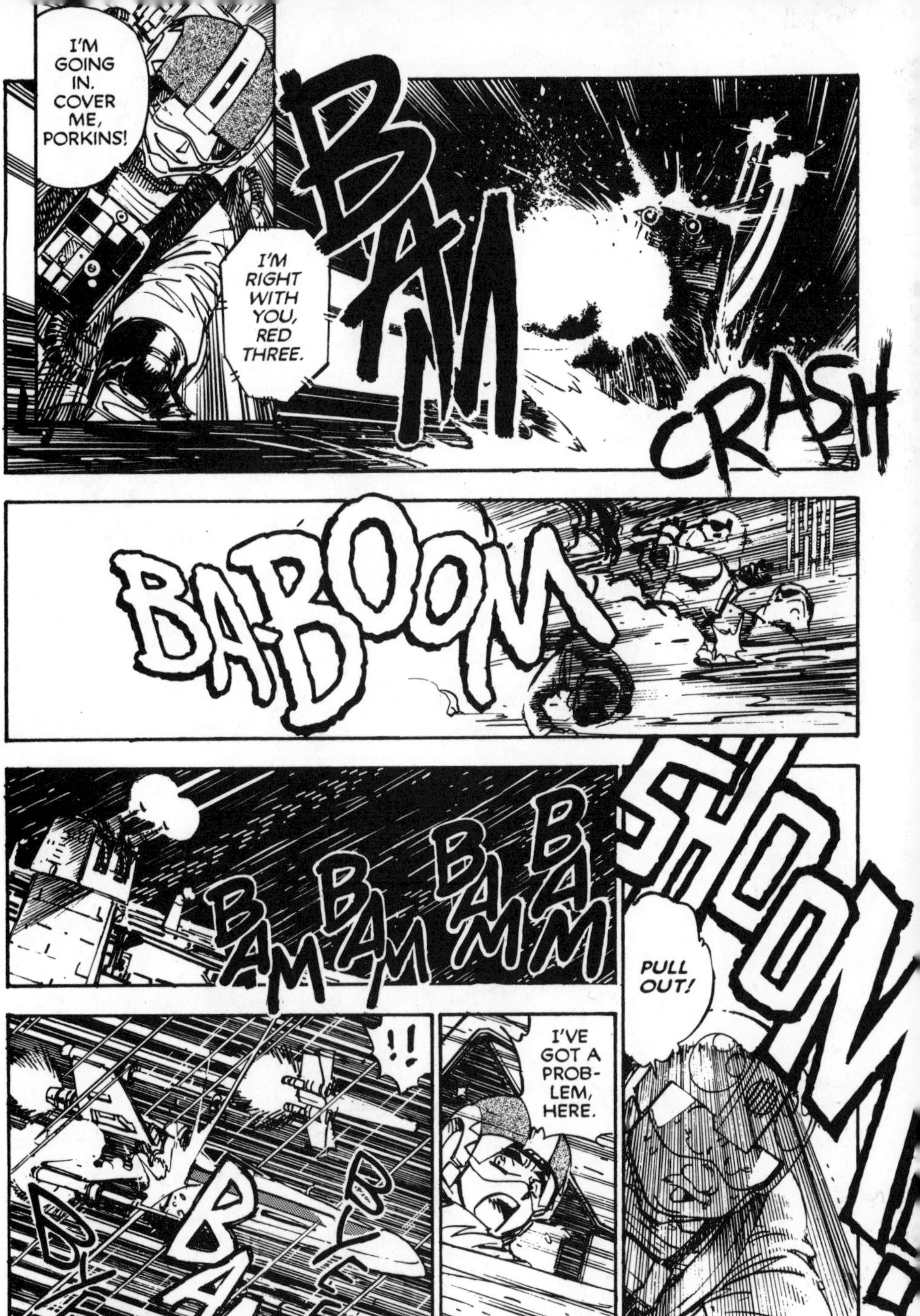
I'M GOING IN. COVER ME, PORKINS!
I'M RIGHT WITH YOU, RED THREE.
BAM
CRASH
BA-DOOM
SHOOM!!
PULL OUT!
!!
BAM!
I'VE GOT A PROB-LEM, HERE.

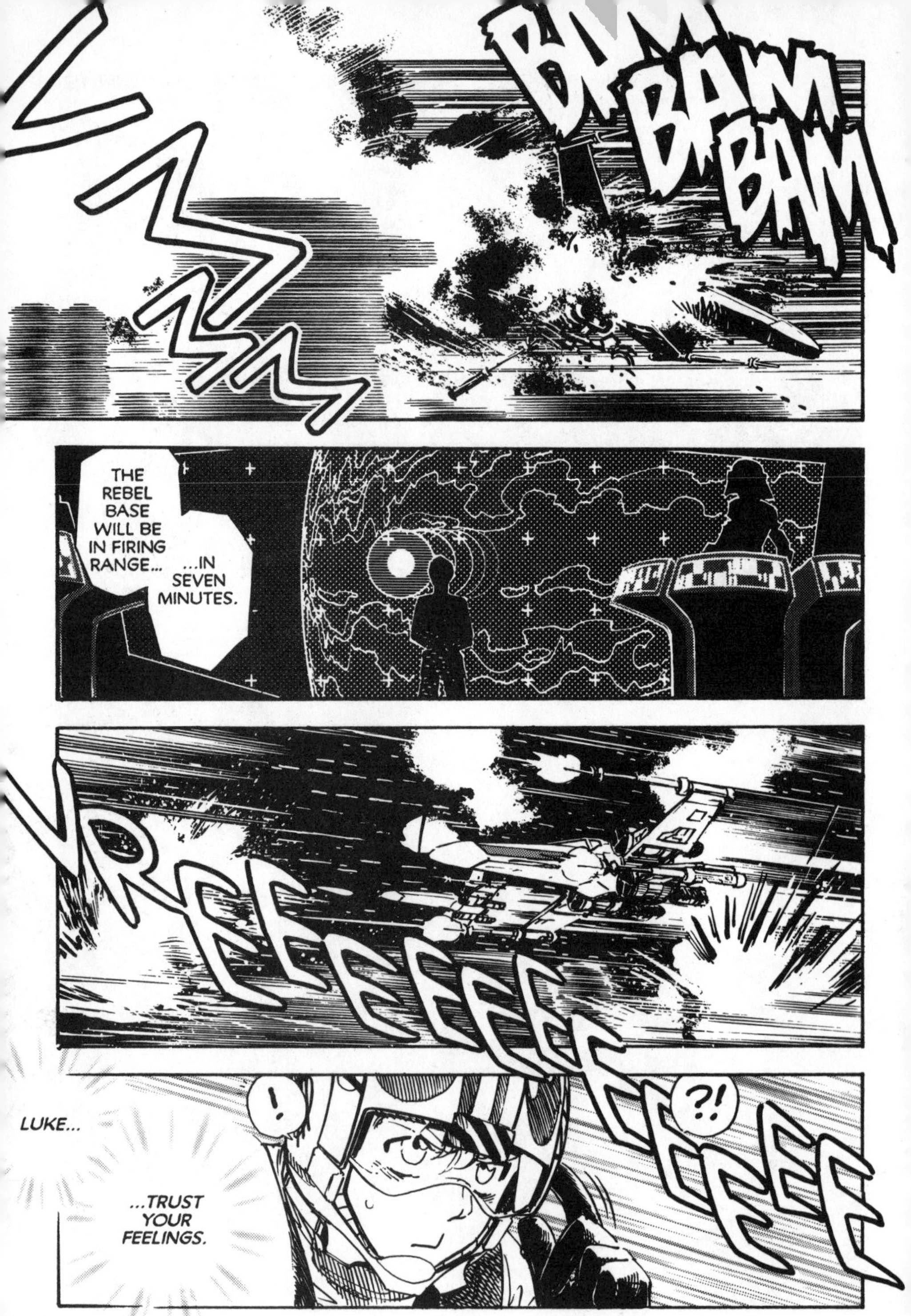
VMMMM
BAM BAM BAM
THE REBEL BASE WILL BE IN FIRING RANGE...
...IN SEVEN MINUTES.
VREEEEEEEEEEEEEEE
!
?!
LUKE...
...TRUST YOUR FEELINGS.

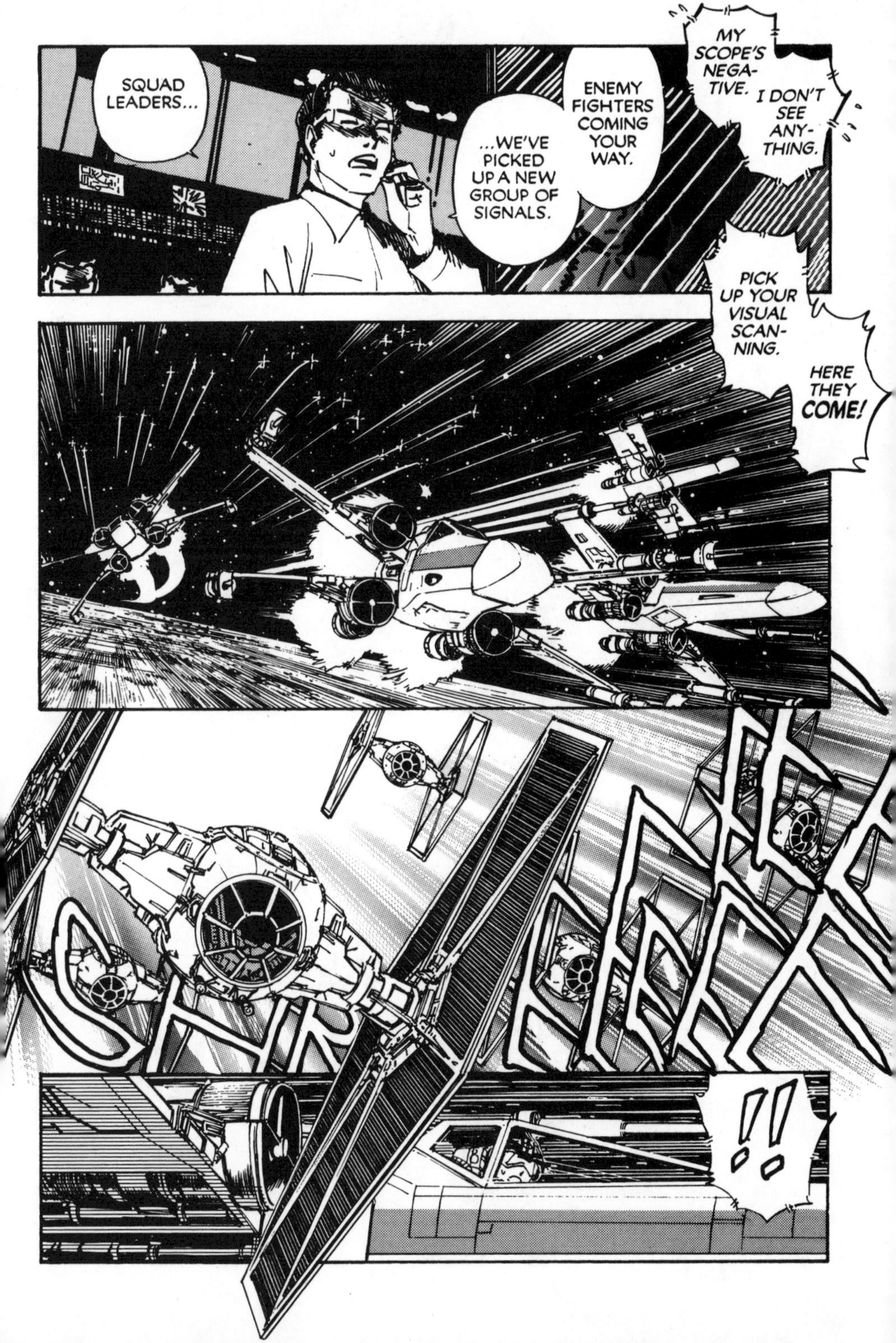
SQUAD LEADERS...
...WE'VE PICKED UP A NEW GROUP OF SIGNALS.
ENEMY FIGHTERS COMING YOUR WAY.
MY SCOPE'S NEGATIVE.
I DON'T SEE ANYTHING.
PICK UP YOUR VISUAL SCANNING.
HERE THEY COME!
!!

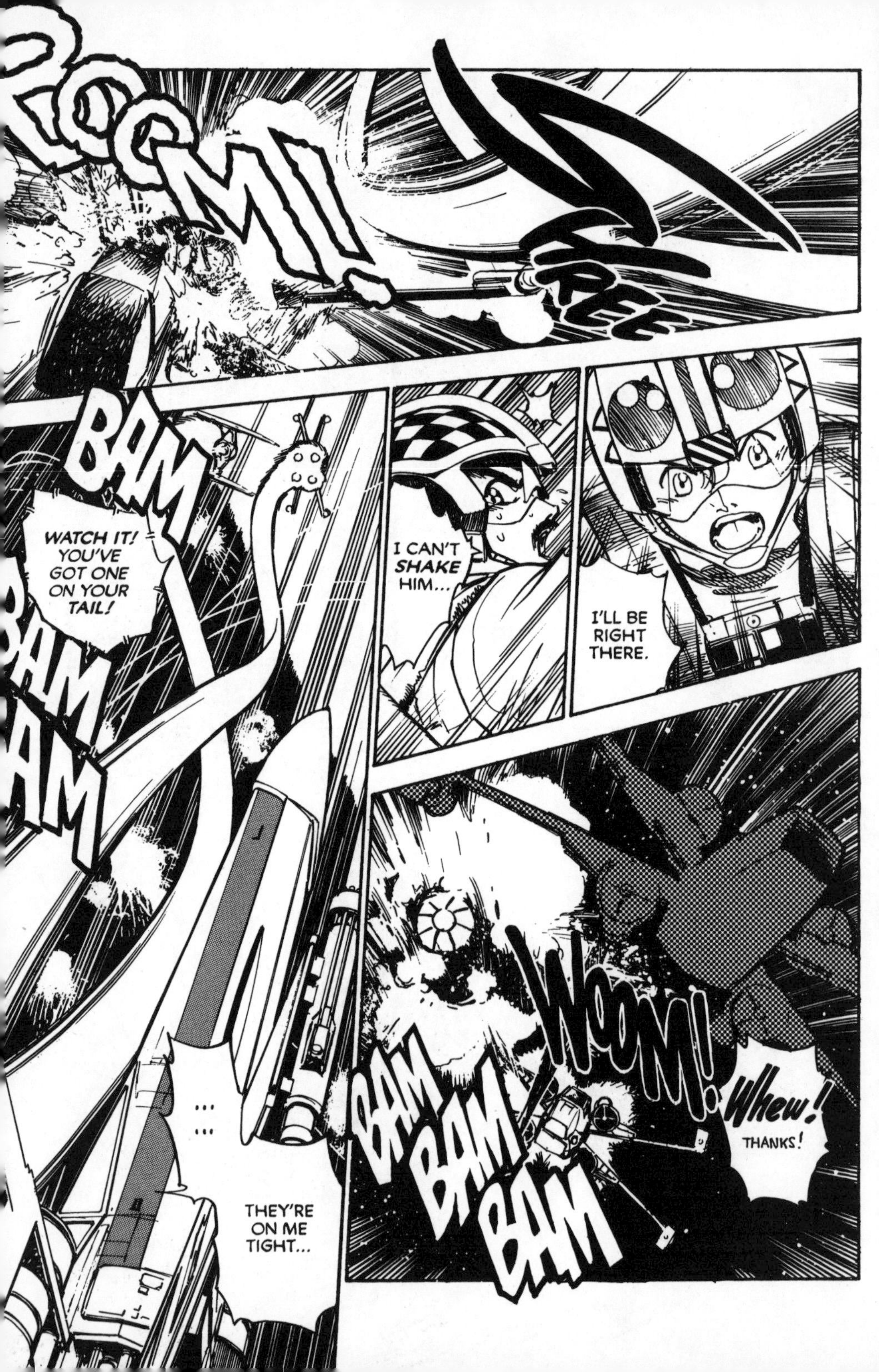
BOOM!
BAM
BAM
BAM
BAM
WATCH IT! YOU'VE GOT ONE ON YOUR TAIL!
I CAN'T SHAKE HIM...
I'LL BE RIGHT THERE.
...
...
THEY'RE ON ME TIGHT...
BAM
BAM
BAM
WOOM!
Whew!
THANKS!

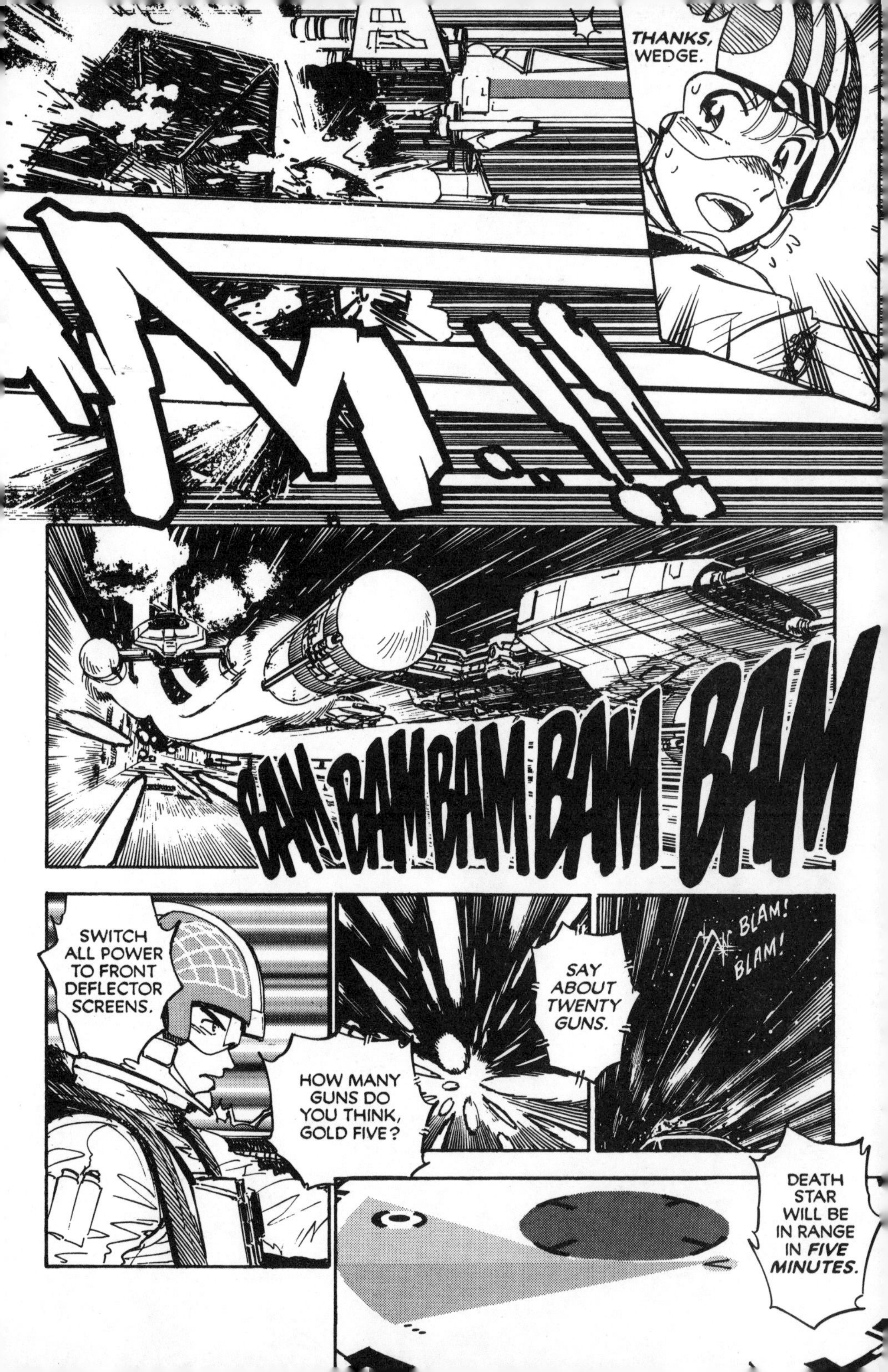

THANKS, WEDGE.
BAM BAM BAM BAM BAM
SWITCH ALL POWER TO FRONT DEFLECTOR SCREENS.
HOW MANY GUNS DO YOU THINK, GOLD FIVE?
SAY ABOUT TWENTY GUNS.
BLAM! BLAM!
DEATH STAR WILL BE IN RANGE IN *FIVE MINUTES.*

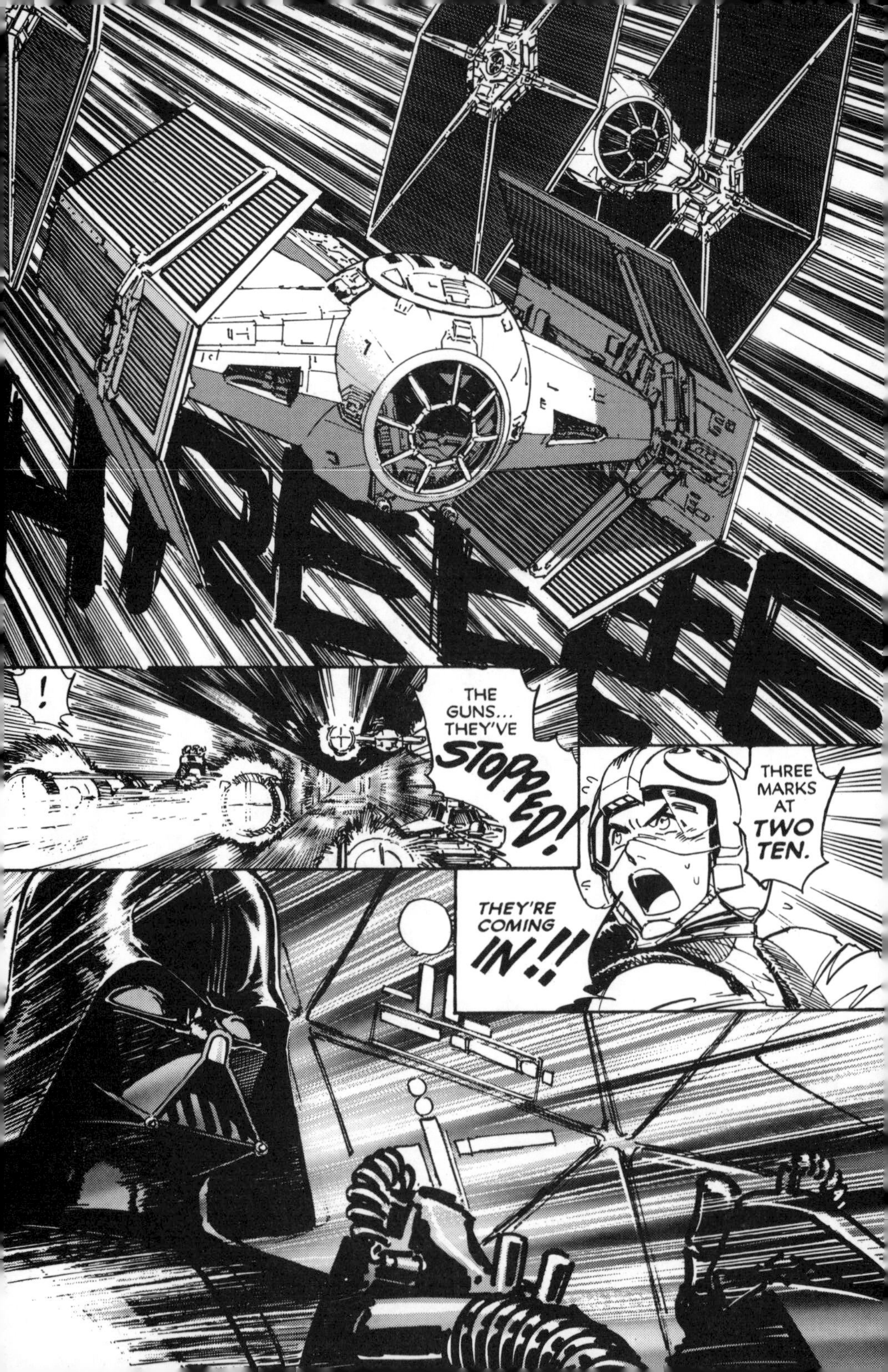
!
THE GUNS... THEY'VE STOPPED!
THREE MARKS AT TWO TEN.
THEY'RE COMING IN!!

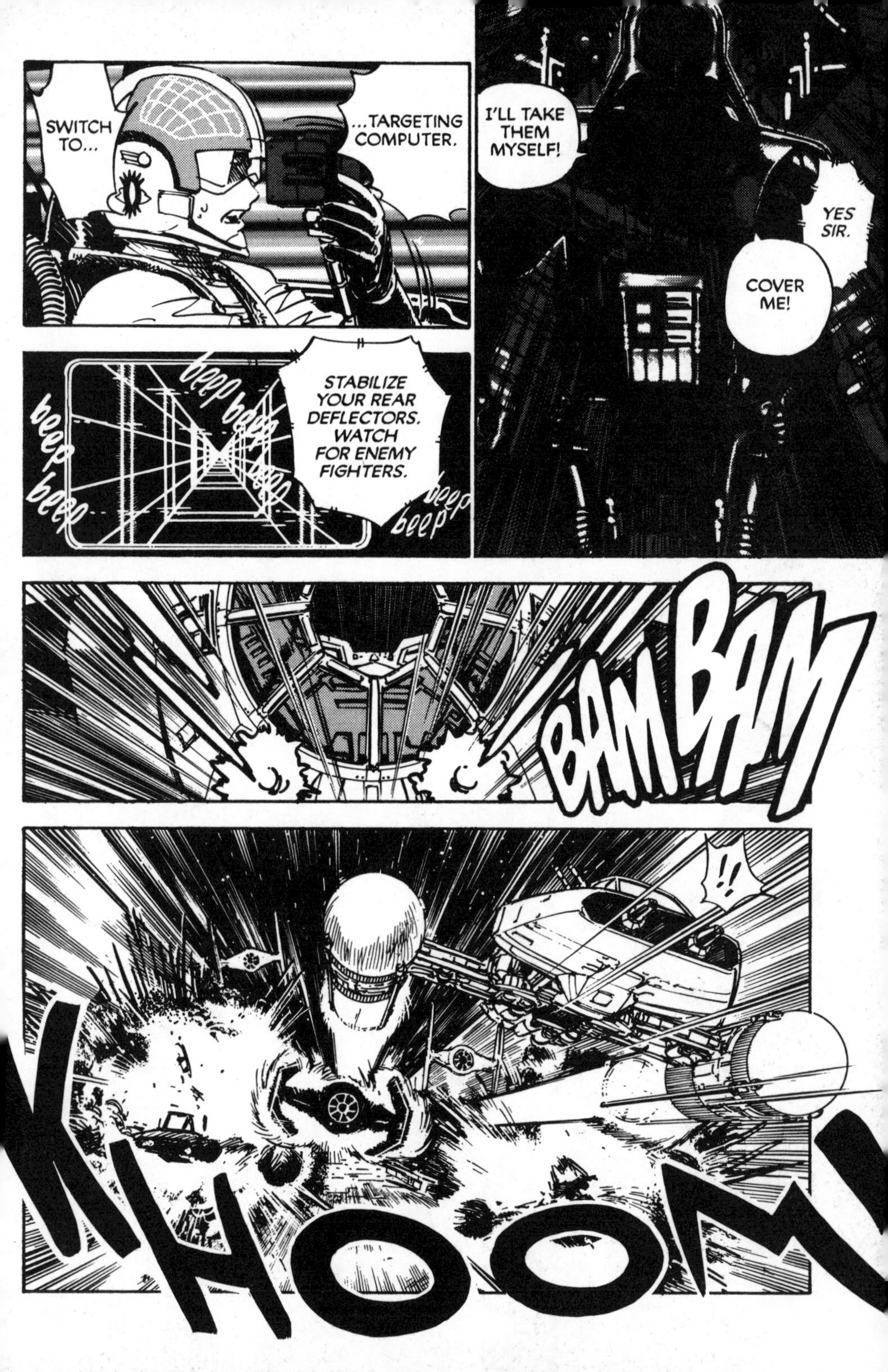
SWITCH TO...
...TARGETING COMPUTER.
beep beep
beep beep
STABILIZE YOUR REAR DEFLECTORS. WATCH FOR ENEMY FIGHTERS.
beep beep
I'LL TAKE THEM MYSELF!
COVER ME!
YES SIR.
BAM BAM
!!
WHOOM

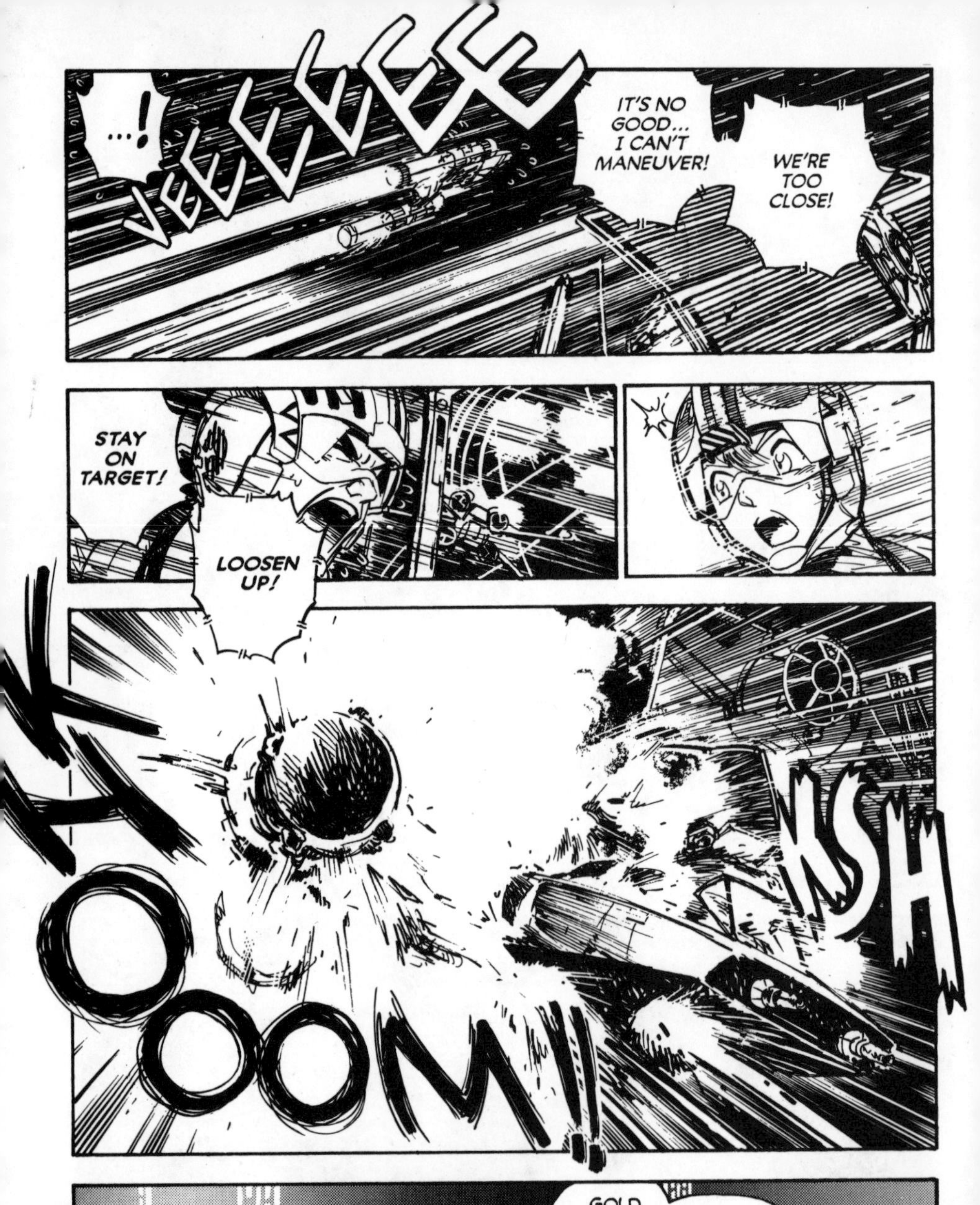
...!
VEEEEEE
IT'S NO GOOD... I CAN'T MANEUVER!
WE'RE TOO CLOSE!
STAY ON TARGET!
LOOSEN UP!
KA
BOOOOM!!
KSH
GOLD FIVE TO RED LEADER...
LOST TIREE, LOST HUTCH.

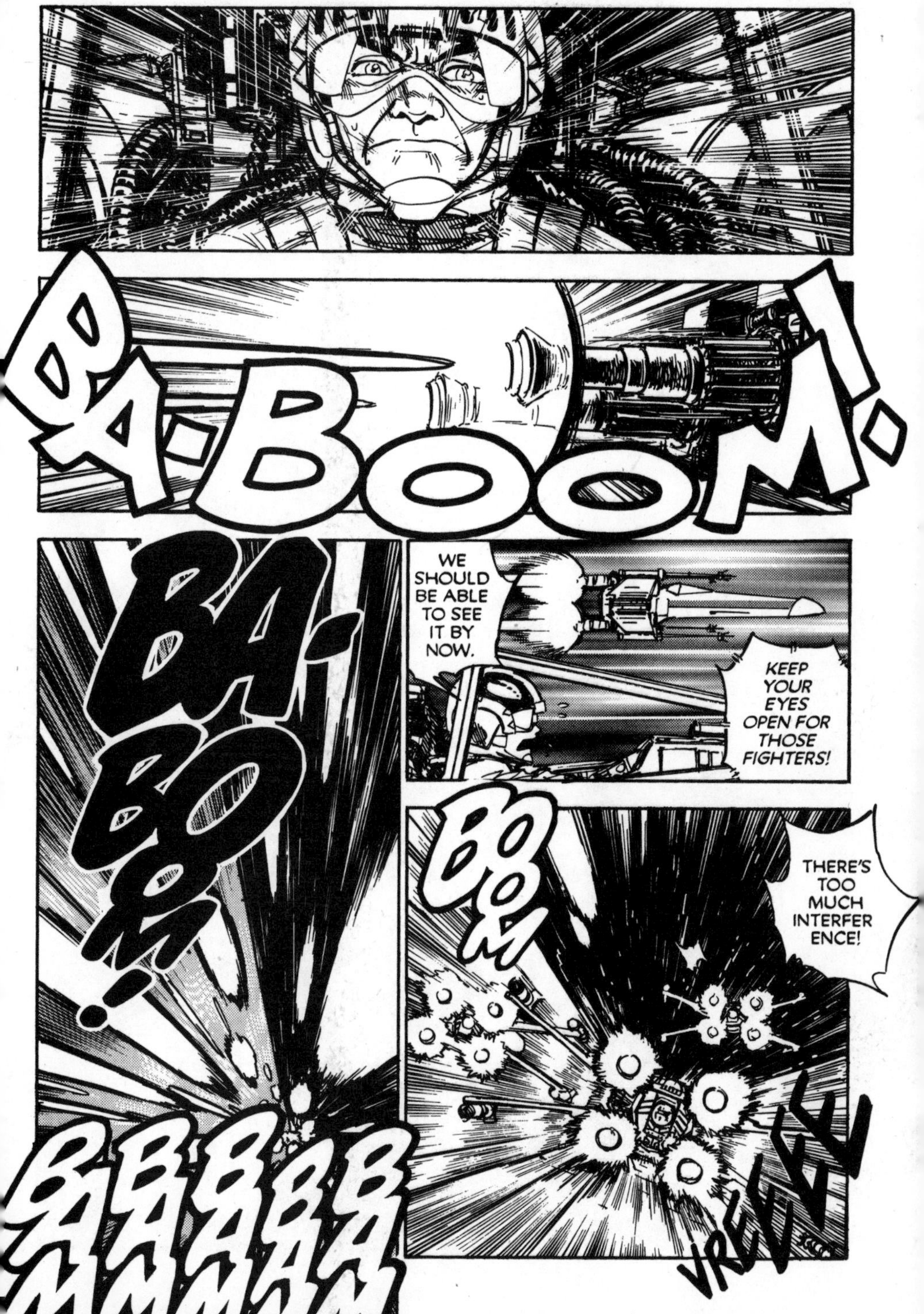
BA-BOOM!
BA-BOOM!
BAM BAM BAM BAM BAM BAM
WE SHOULD BE ABLE TO SEE IT BY NOW.
KEEP YOUR EYES OPEN FOR THOSE FIGHTERS!
BOOOM
THERE'S TOO MUCH INTERFERENCE!
VREEEE

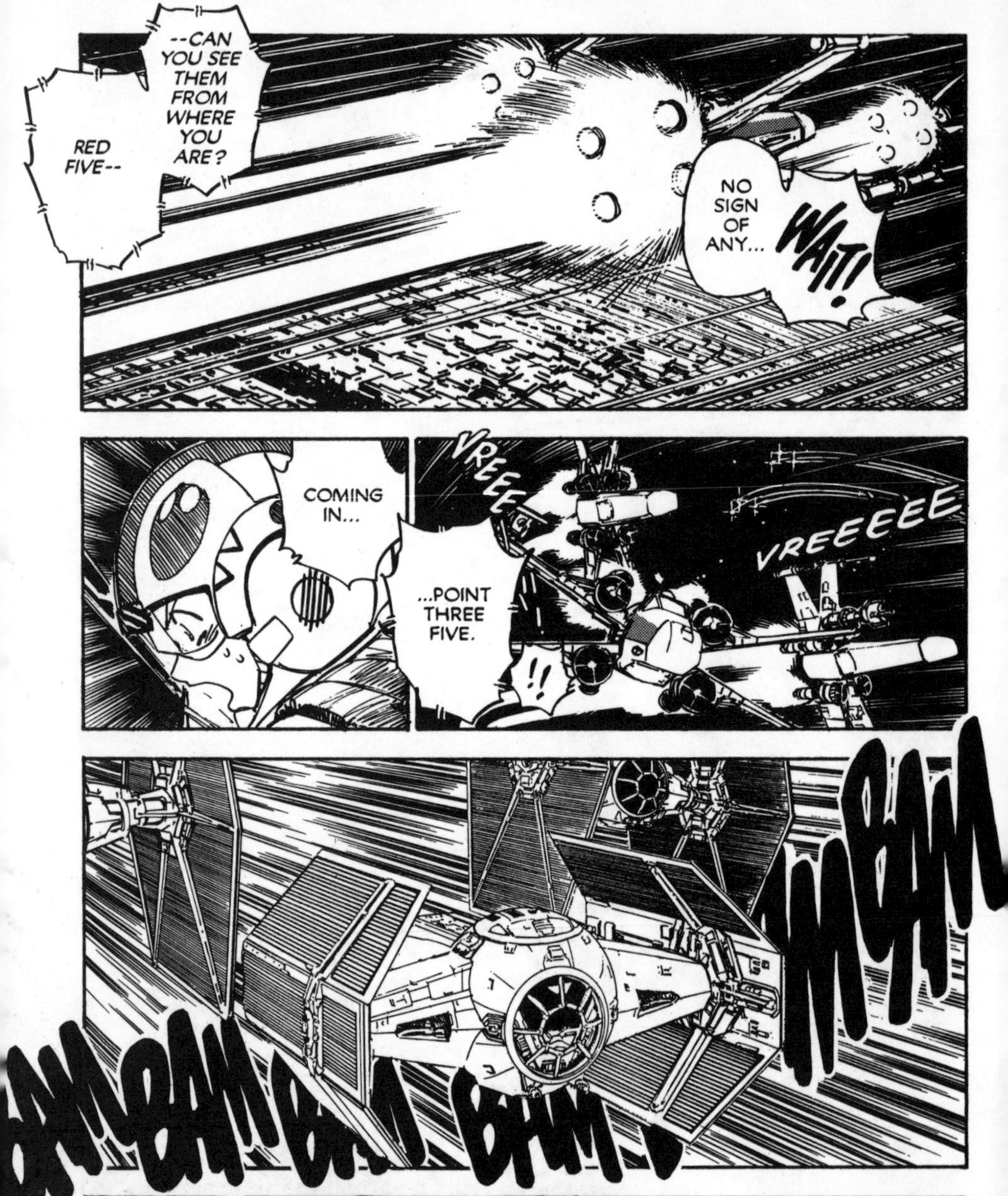
RED FIVE--
--CAN YOU SEE THEM FROM WHERE YOU ARE?
NO SIGN OF ANY...
WAIT!
COMING IN...
...POINT THREE FIVE.
VREEE
VREEEEEE
!!
BAM BAM
BAM BAM BAM BAM
KLIK
I SEE THEM.
I'M IN RANGE.
beep
beep
beep

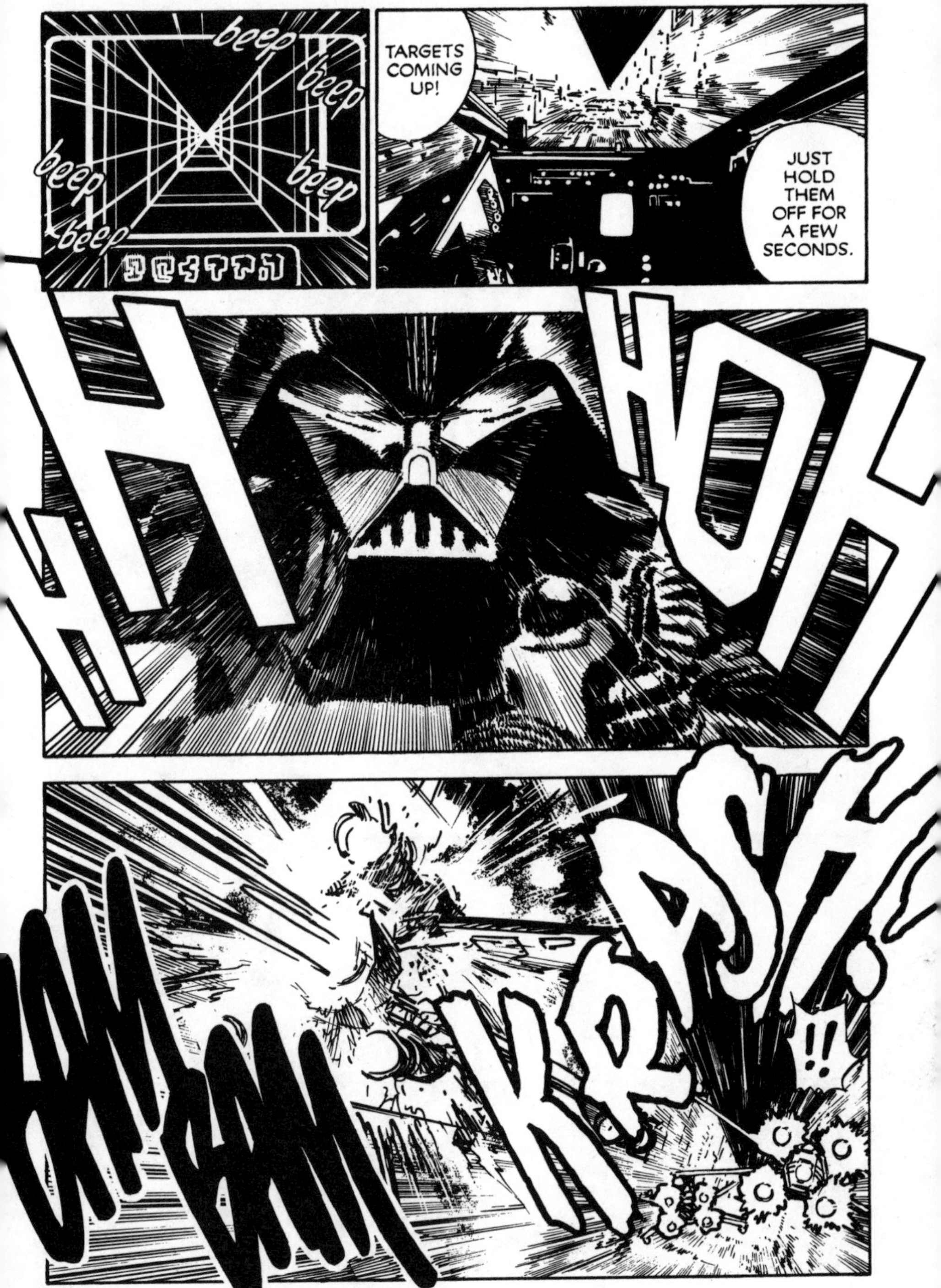
beep
beep
beep
beep
beep
TARGETS COMING UP!
JUST HOLD THEM OFF FOR A FEW SECONDS.
KRASH!!

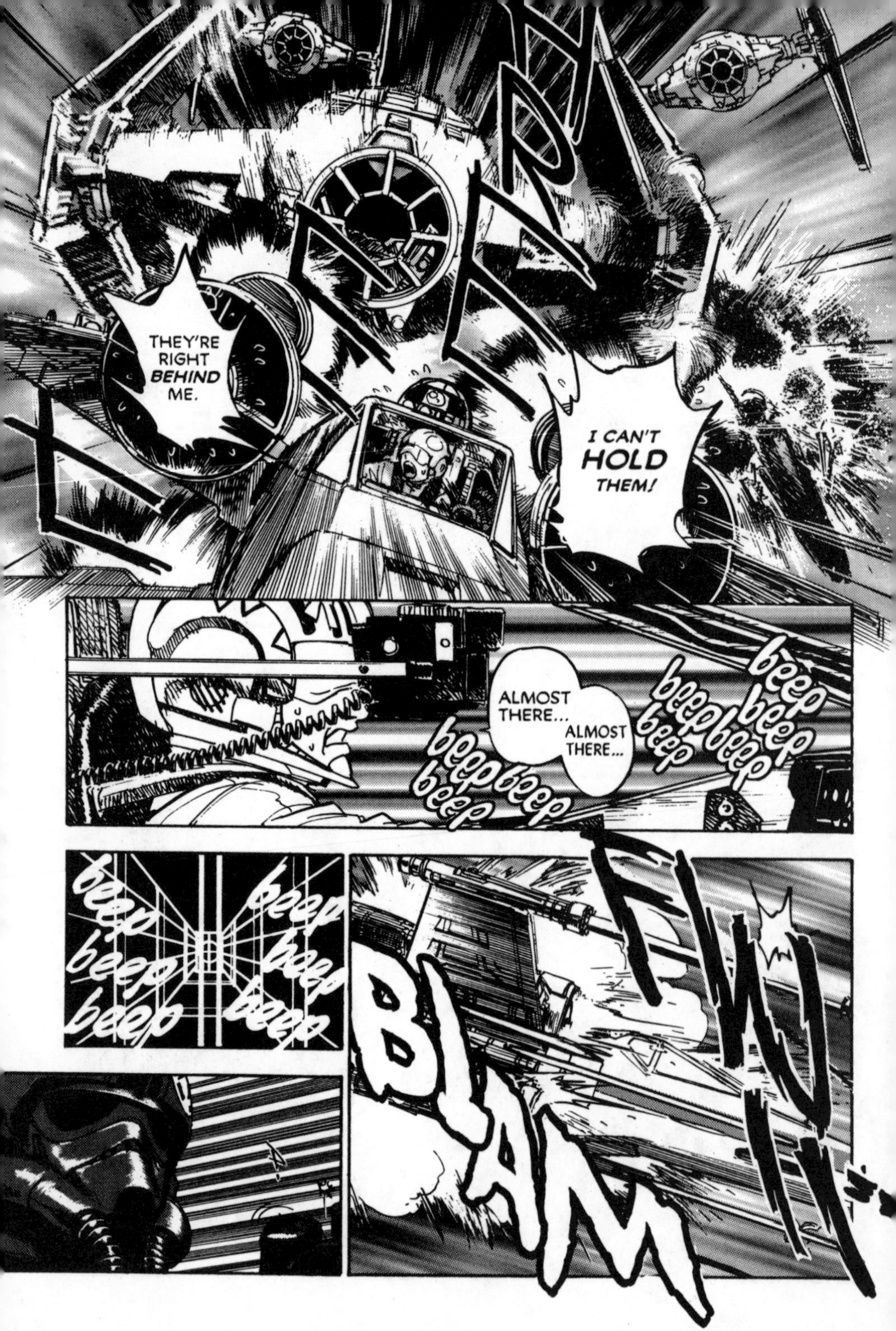
THEY'RE RIGHT *BEHIND* ME.
I CAN'T **HOLD** THEM!
ALMOST THERE...
ALMOST THERE...
beep beep beep beep beep
beep beep beep
beep beep beep
beep beep beep
BLAM

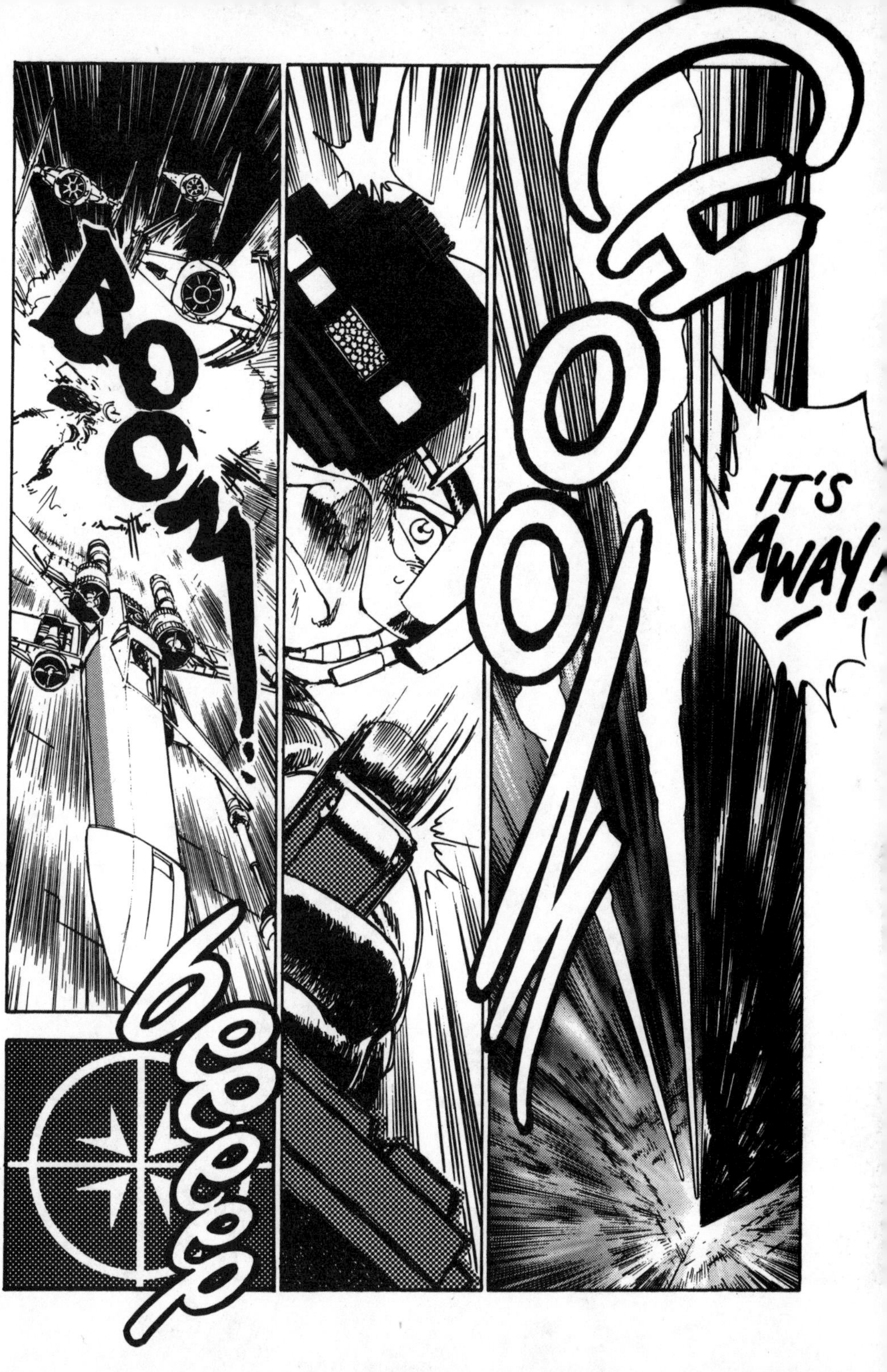
BOOM!
WOOOOP
CHOOOM
IT'S AWAY!

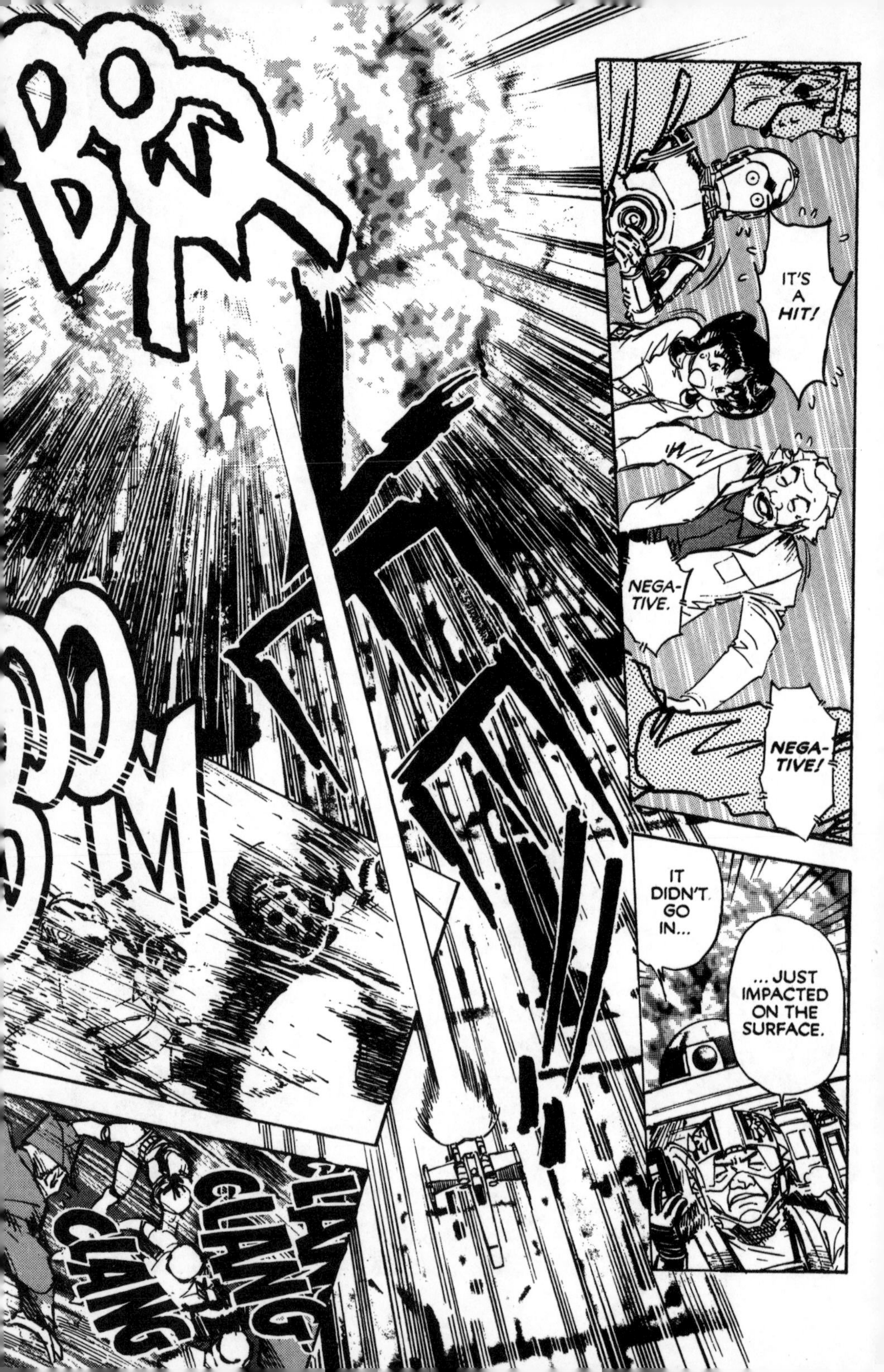
CLANG
CLANG
IT'S A HIT!
NEGA-TIVE.
NEGA-TIVE!
IT DIDN'T GO IN...
... JUST IMPACTED ON THE SURFACE.

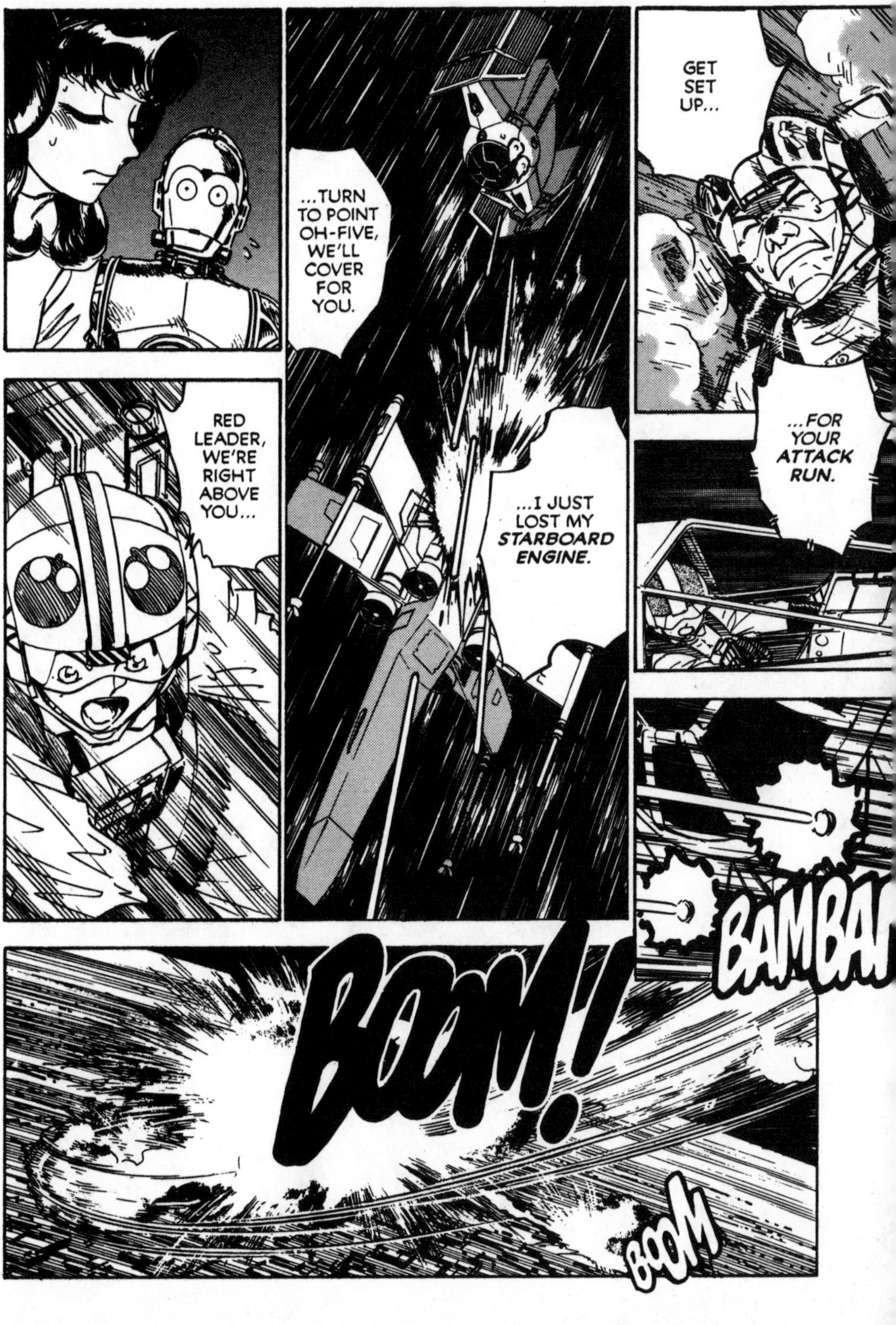

RED LEADER, WE'RE RIGHT ABOVE YOU...
...TURN TO POINT OH-FIVE, WE'LL COVER FOR YOU.
...I JUST LOST MY *STARBOARD ENGINE.*
GET SET UP...
...FOR YOUR *ATTACK RUN.*
BAMBA
BOOM!
BOOM

REBEL BASE...

...ONE MINUTE AND CLOSING.

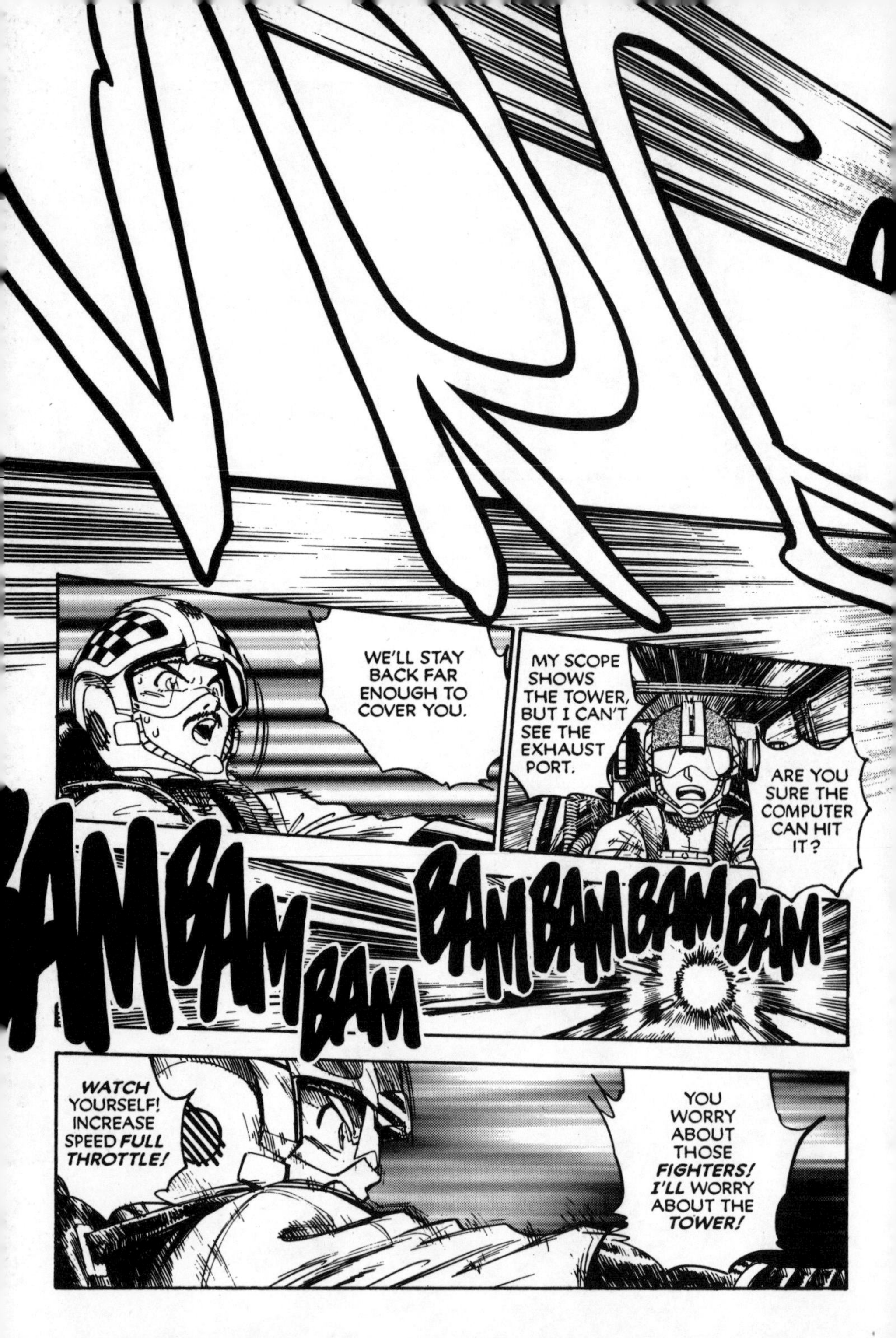
WE'LL STAY BACK FAR ENOUGH TO COVER YOU.
MY SCOPE SHOWS THE TOWER, BUT I CAN'T SEE THE EXHAUST PORT.
ARE YOU SURE THE COMPUTER CAN HIT IT?
BAM BAM BAM
BAM BAM BAM BAM
WATCH YOURSELF! INCREASE SPEED *FULL THROTTLE!*
YOU WORRY ABOUT THOSE *FIGHTERS! I'LL* WORRY ABOUT THE *TOWER!*

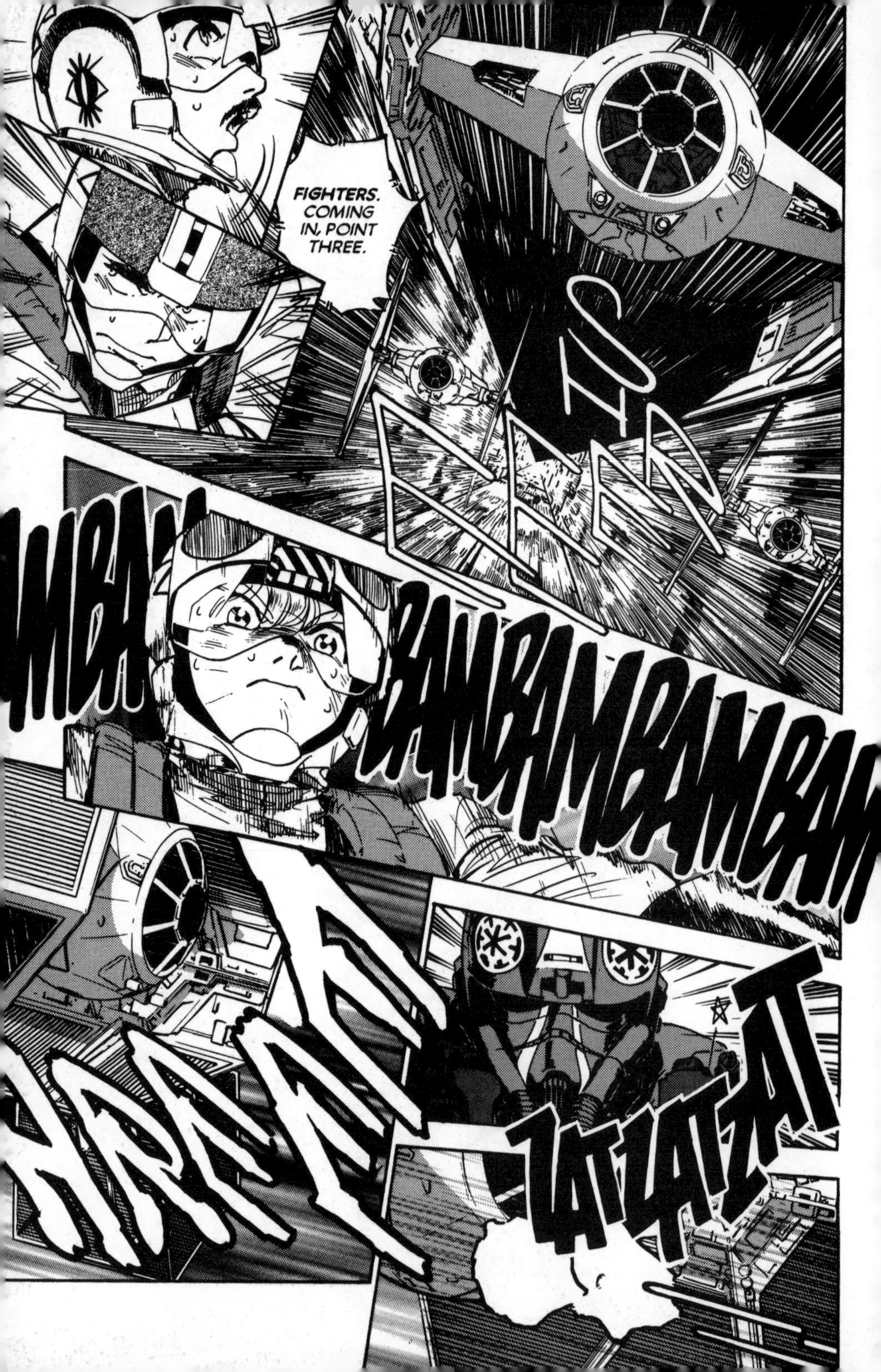
FIGHTERS. COMING IN, POINT THREE.
BAMBAMBAMBAMBAM
ZATZATZAT

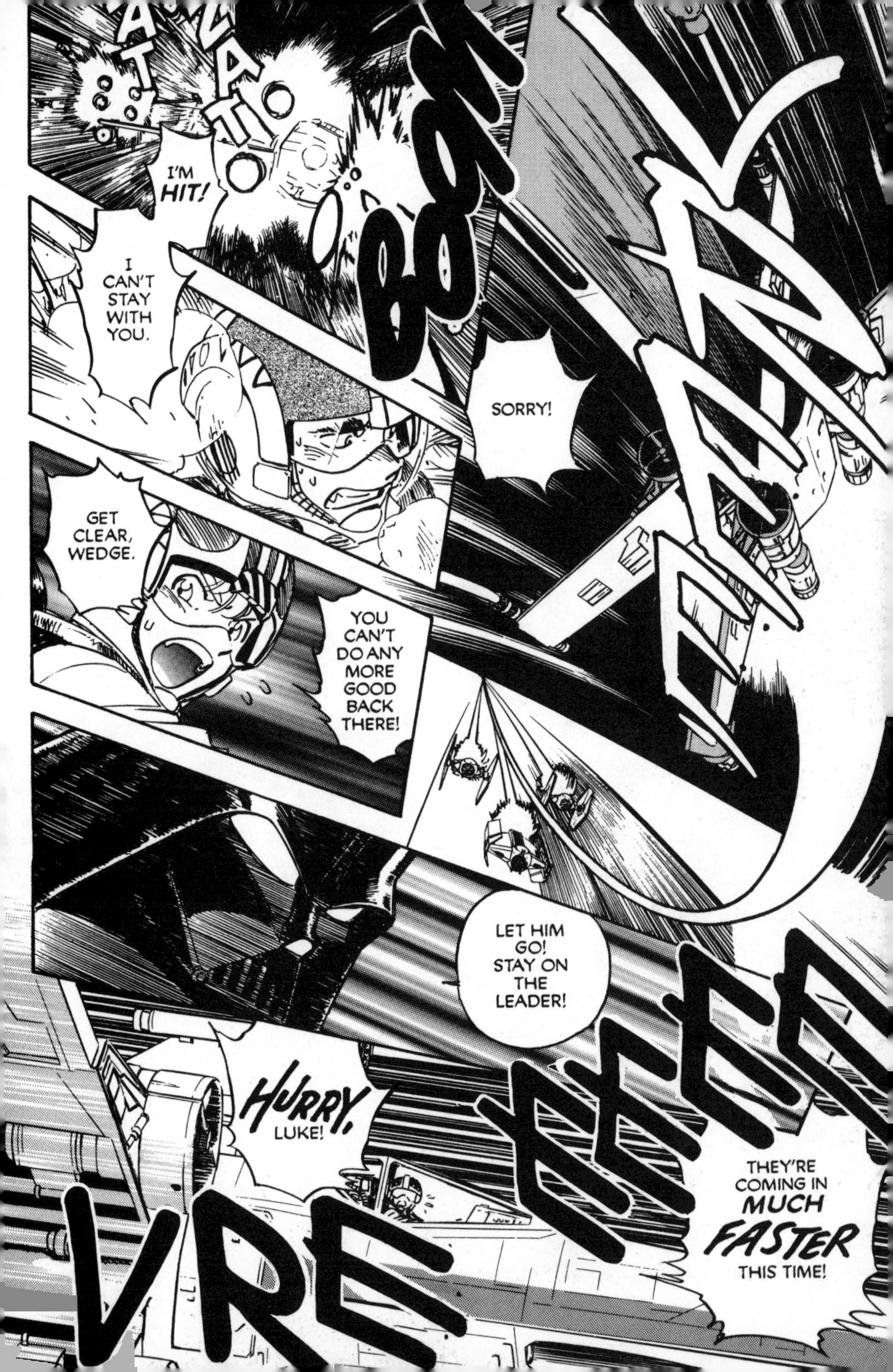

BOOM
I'M HIT!
I CAN'T STAY WITH YOU.
SORRY!
GET CLEAR, WEDGE.
YOU CAN'T DO ANY MORE GOOD BACK THERE!
LET HIM GO! STAY ON THE LEADER!
HURRY, LUKE!
THEY'RE COMING IN MUCH FASTER THIS TIME!

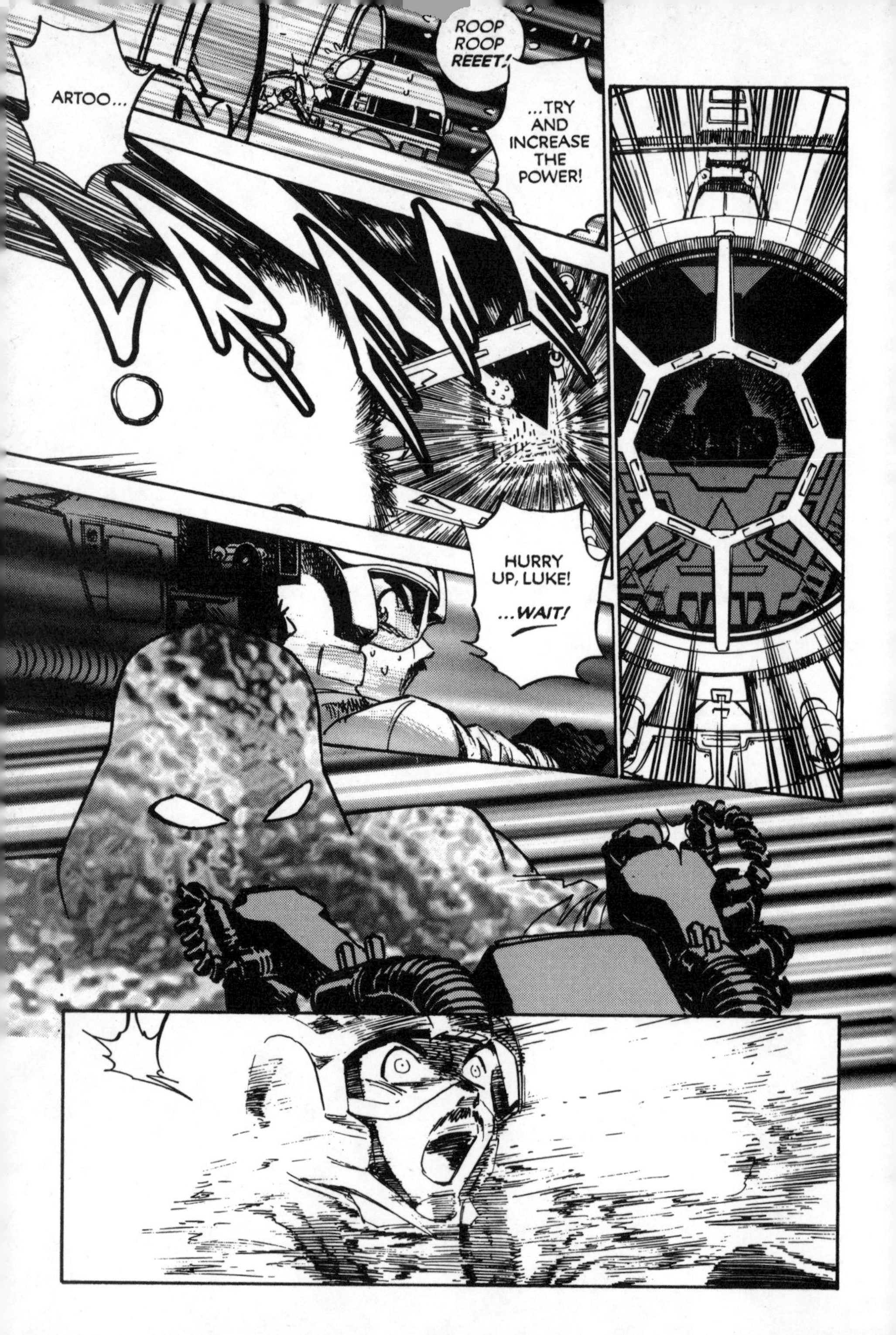
ARTOO...
...TRY AND INCREASE THE POWER!
ROOP ROOP REEET!
HURRY UP, LUKE!
...WAIT!

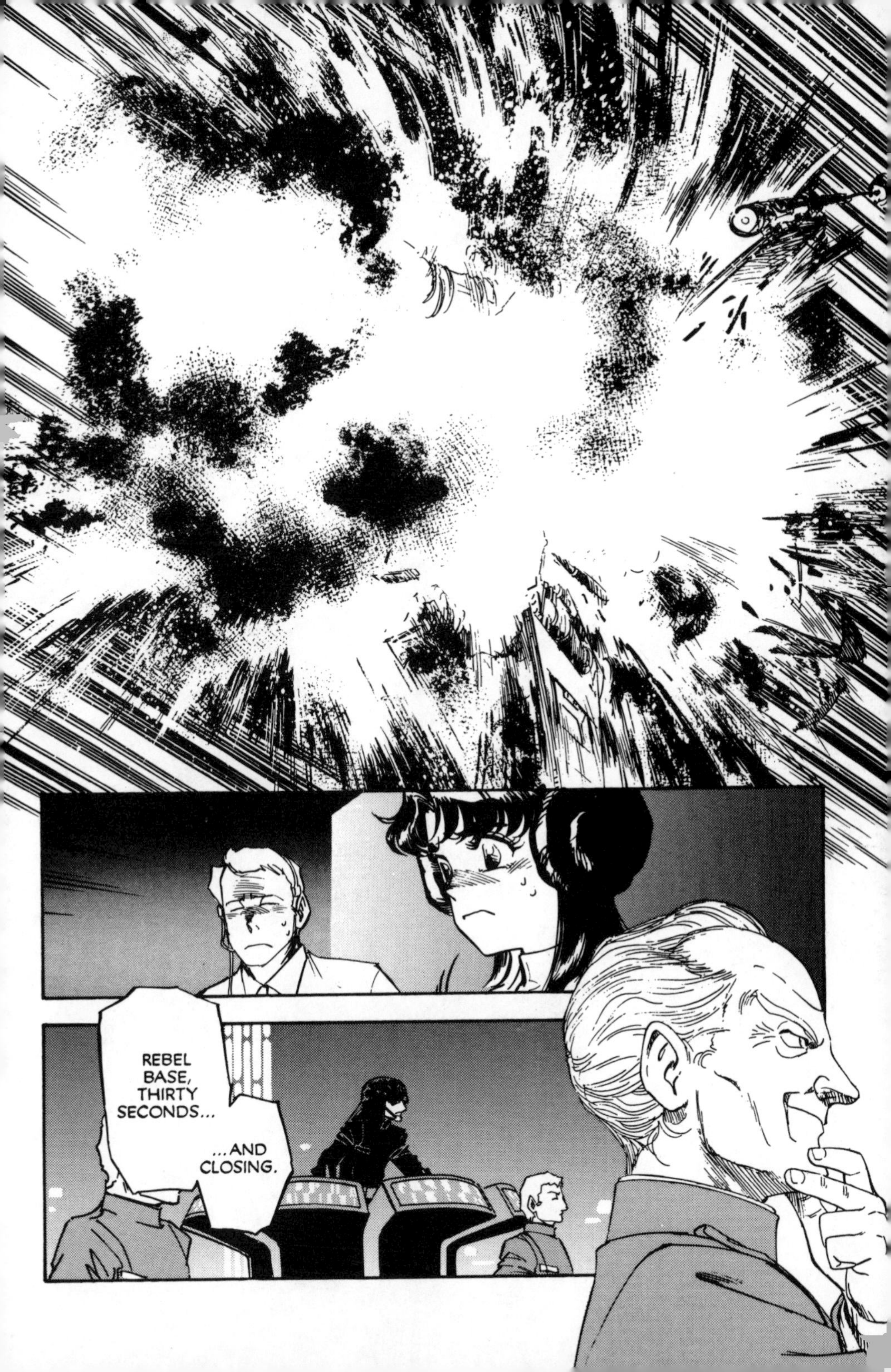
REBEL BASE, THIRTY SECONDS...
...AND CLOSING.

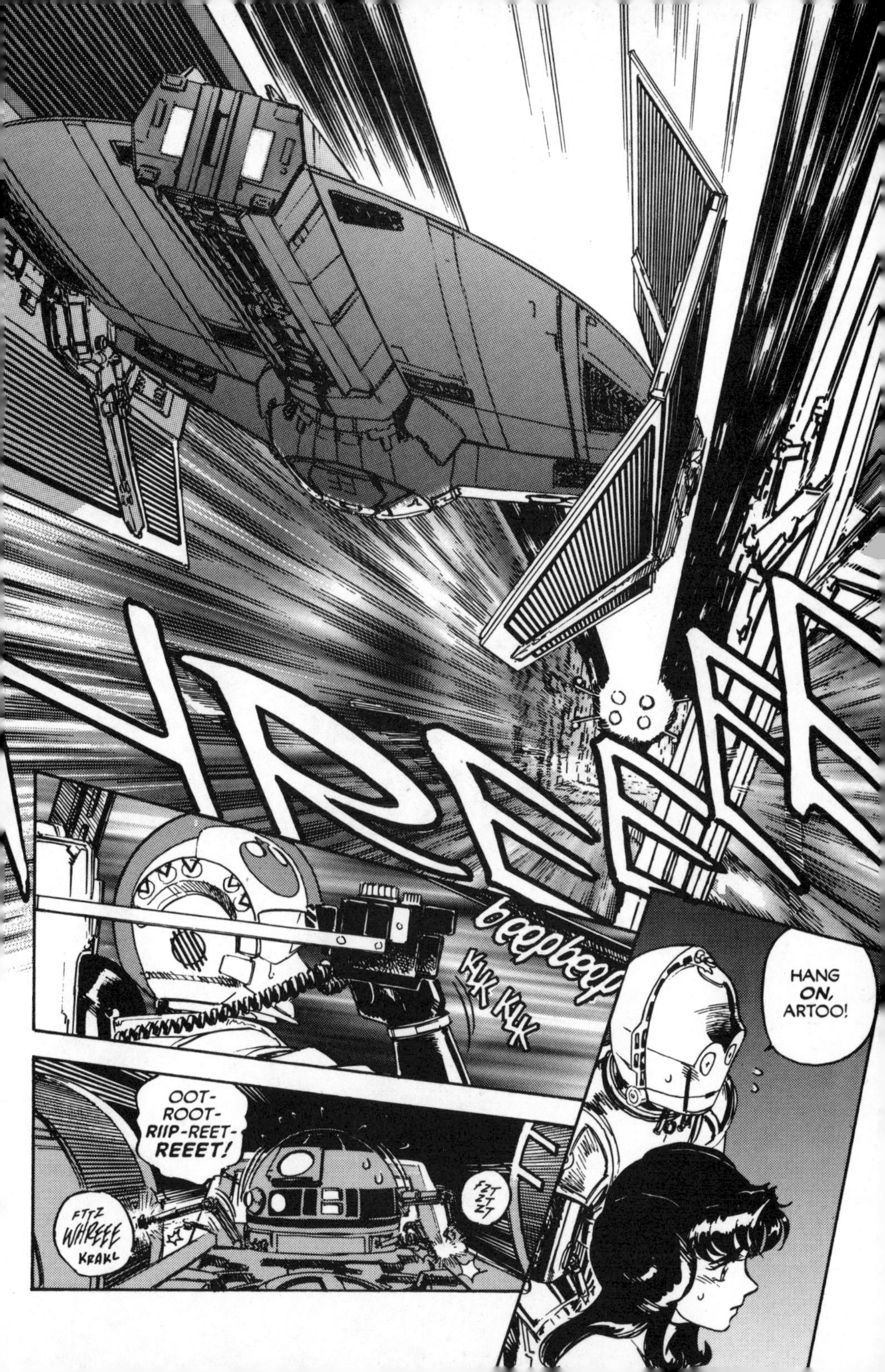
beepbeep
KLIK KLIK
HANG ON, ARTOO!
OOT-ROOT-RIIP-REET-REEET!
FTTZ WHREEE KRAKL
FZT ZT ZT

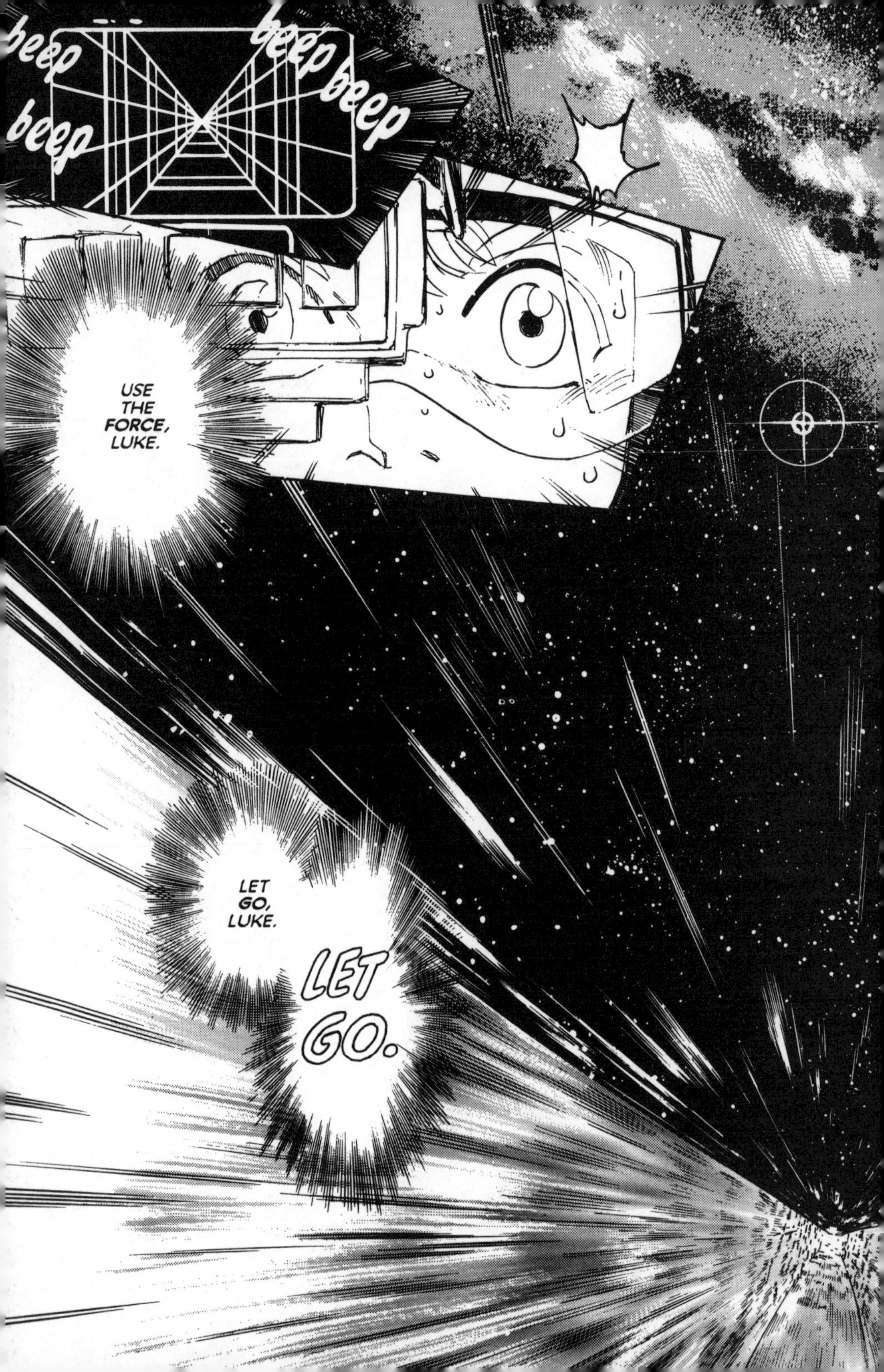
beep
beep
beep beep beep
USE THE FORCE, LUKE.
LET GO, LUKE.
LET GO.

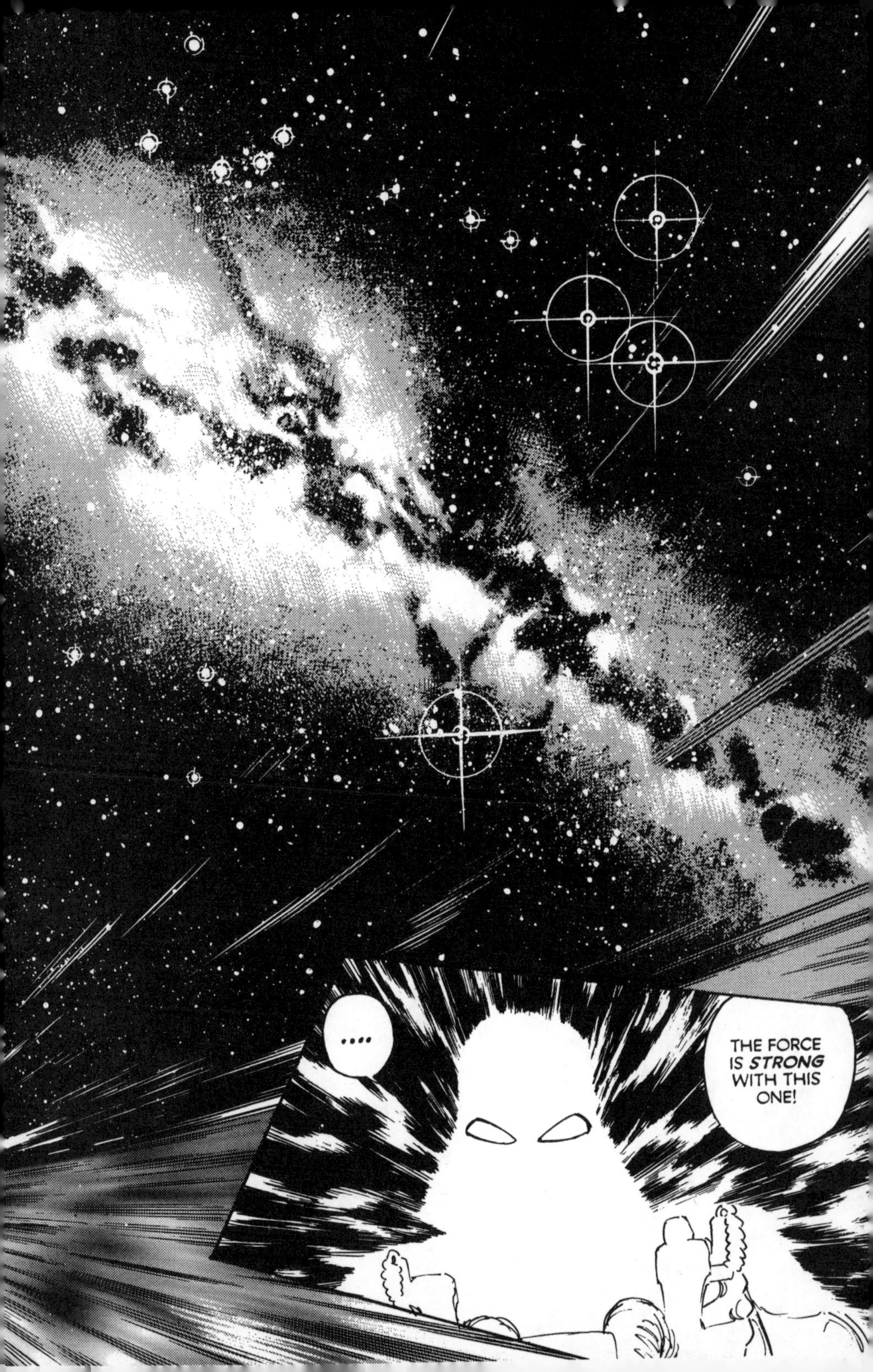
....
THE FORCE IS *STRONG* WITH THIS ONE!

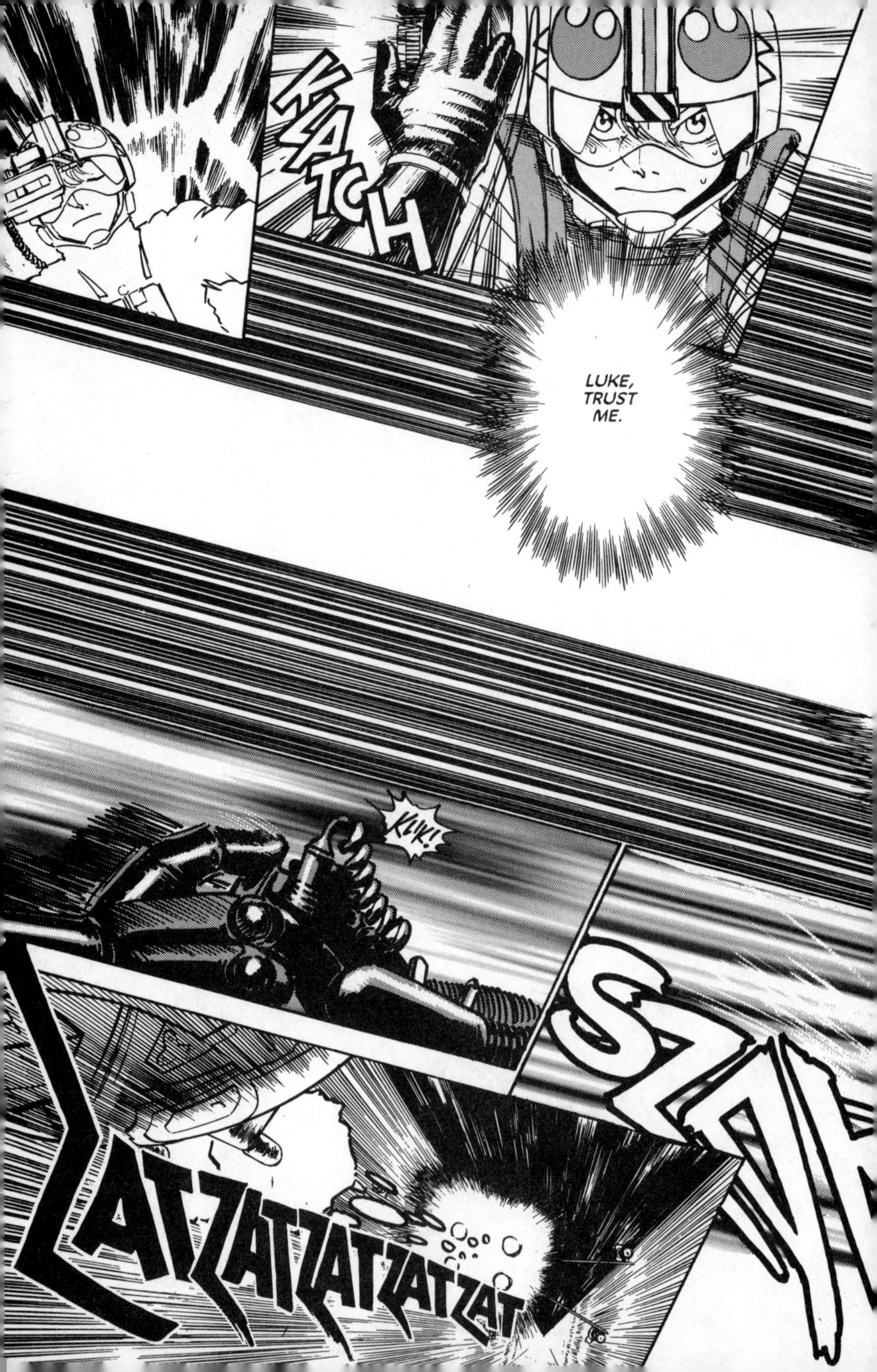
KATCH
LUKE, TRUST ME.
KLIK!
ZATZATZATZATZATZAT

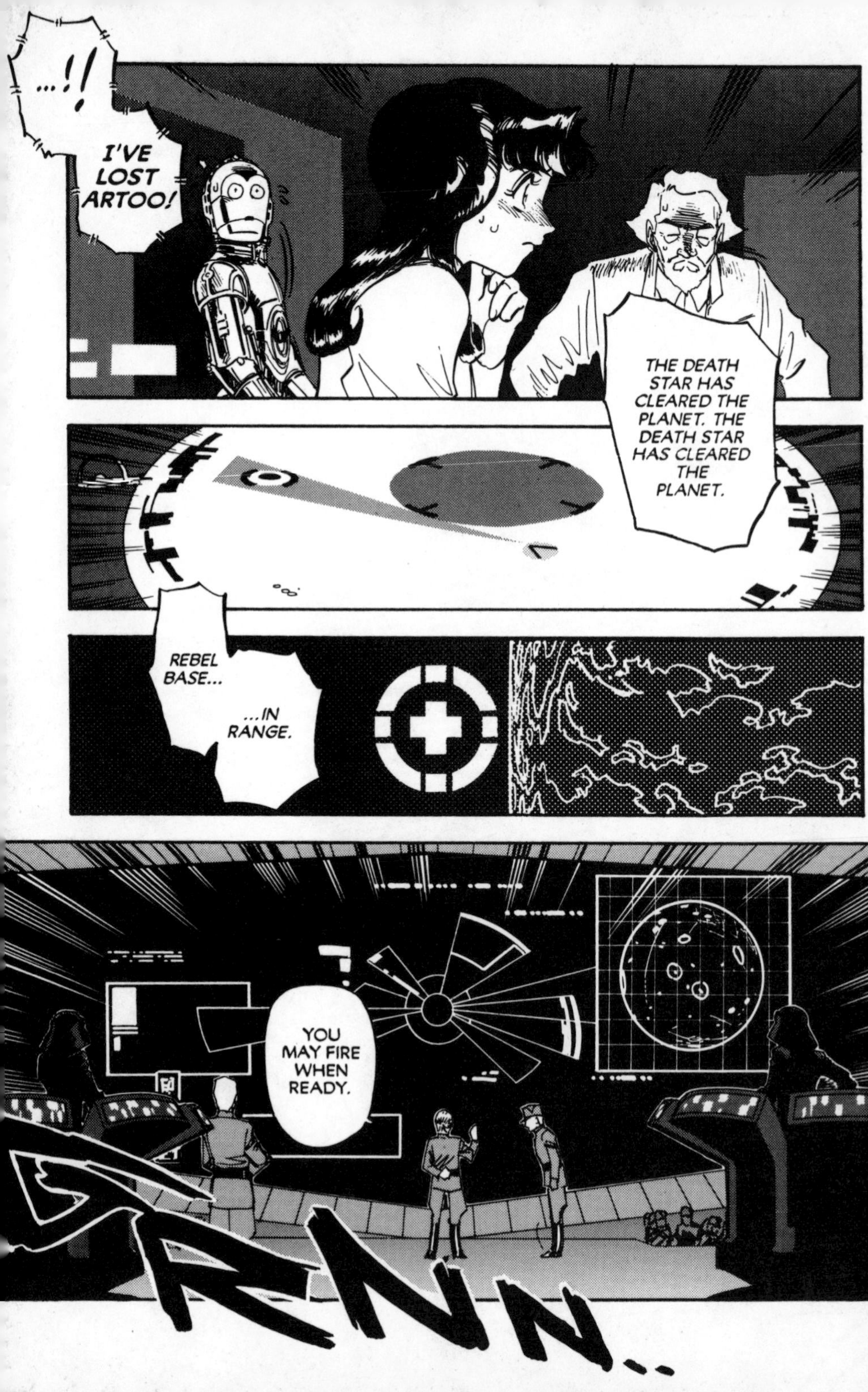
...!!
I'VE LOST ARTOO!
THE DEATH STAR HAS CLEARED THE PLANET. THE DEATH STAR HAS CLEARED THE PLANET.
REBEL BASE...
...IN RANGE.
YOU MAY FIRE WHEN READY.

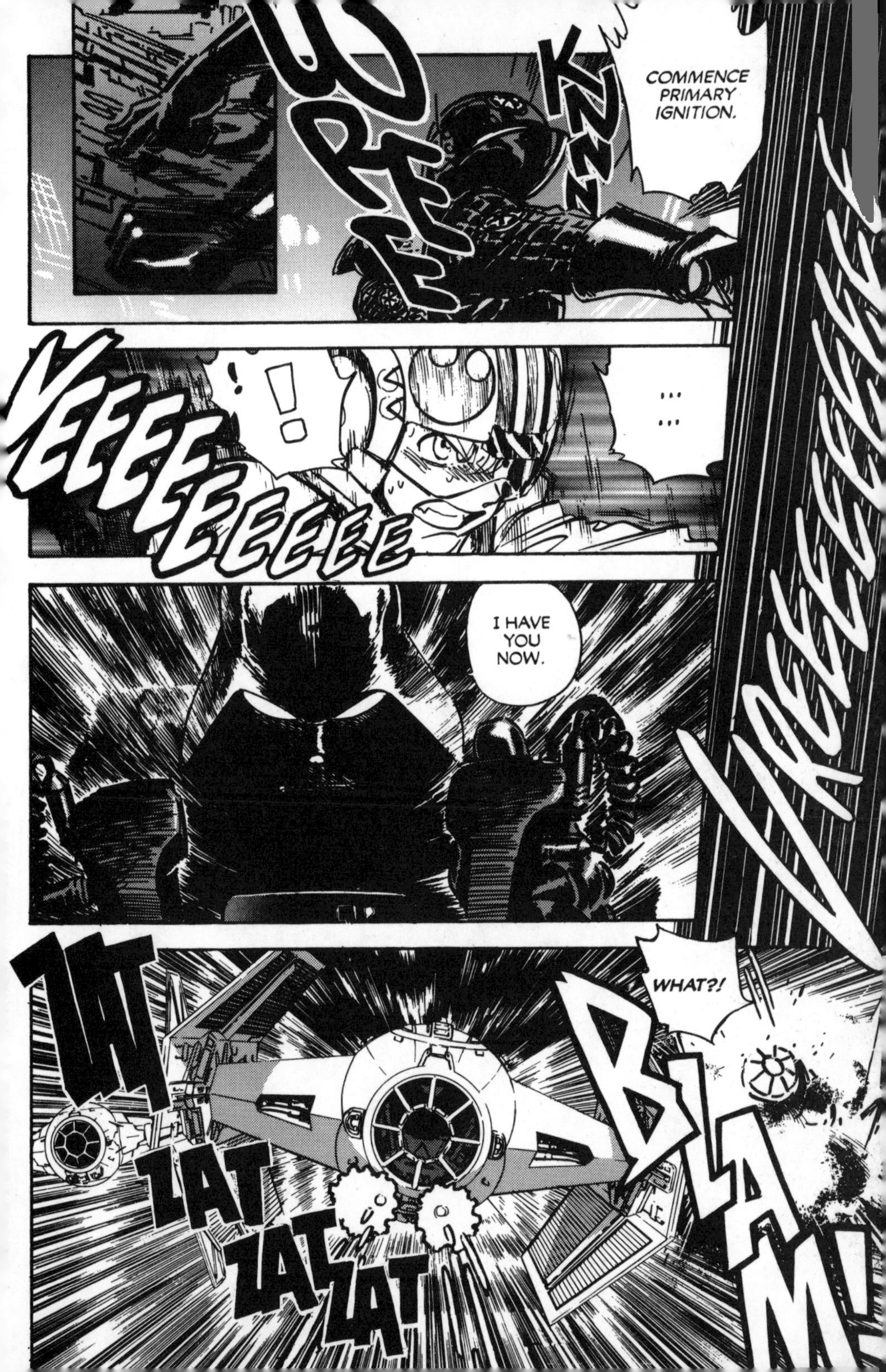
COMMENCE PRIMARY IGNITION.
I HAVE YOU NOW.
ZAT
ZAT
ZAT
ZAT
WHAT?!
BLAM!

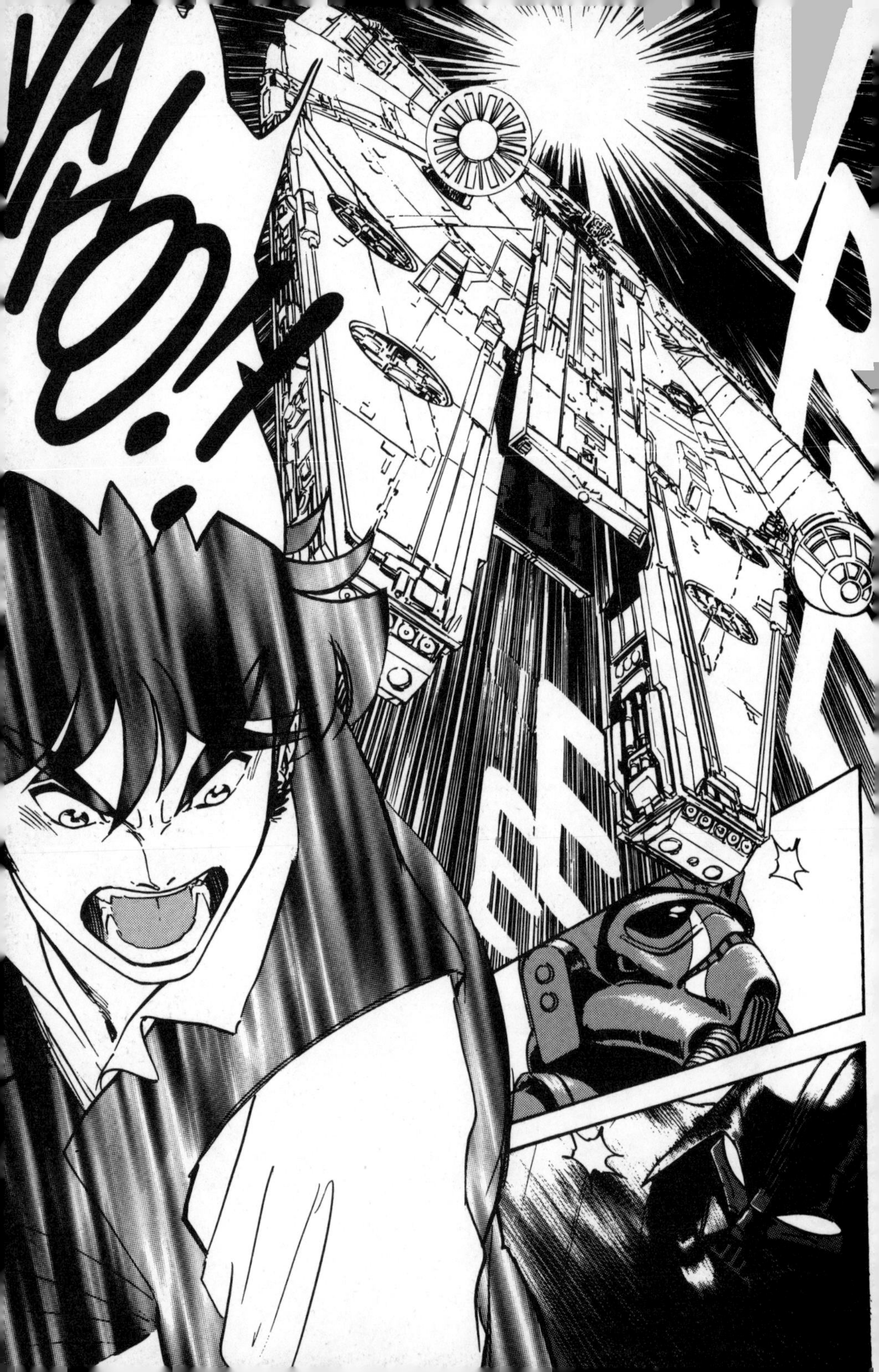
YAHOO!!

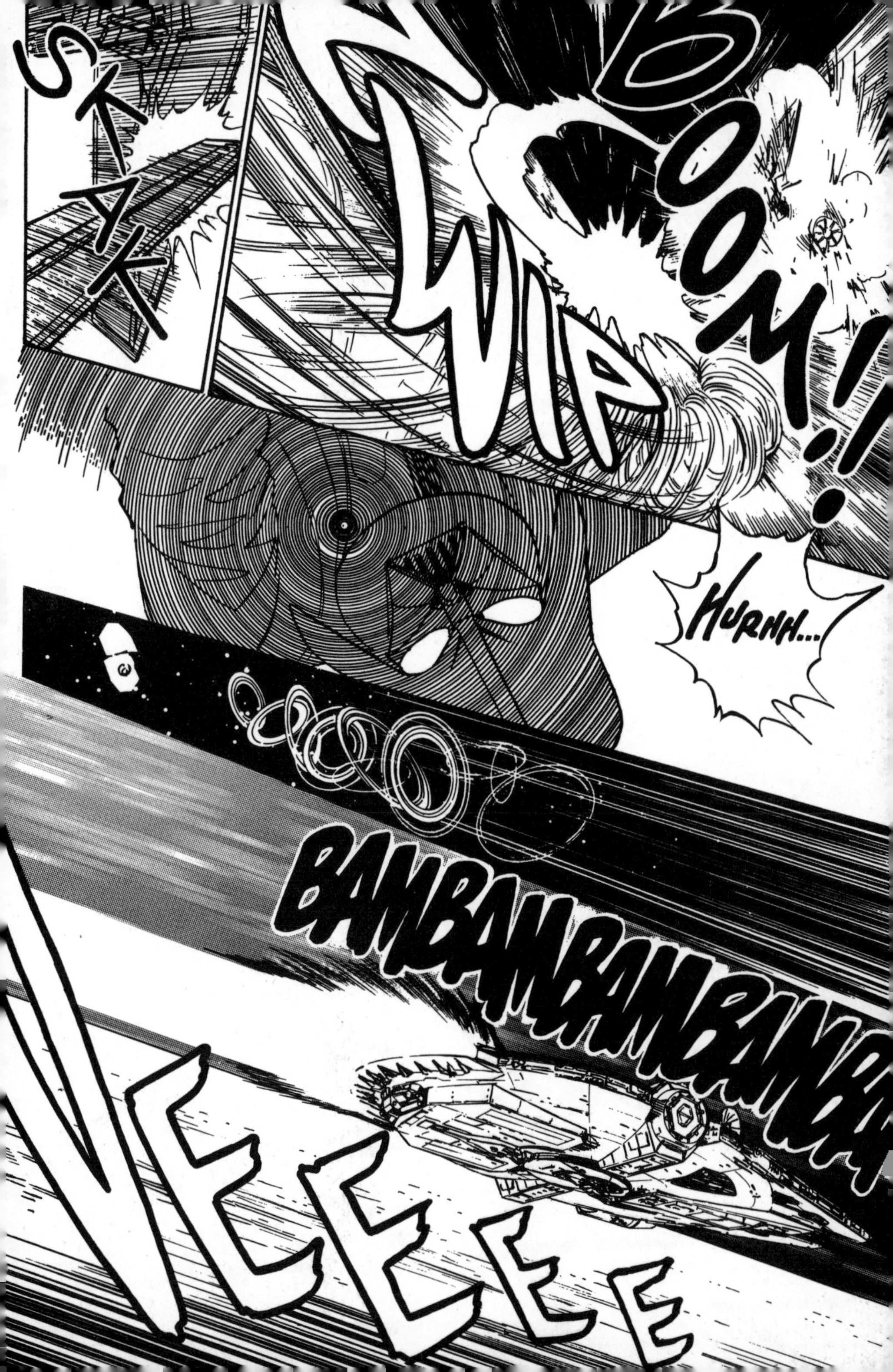
SKAK
ZWIP
DOOOM!!!
HURNH...
BAMBAMBAMBAMBAM
VEEEEE

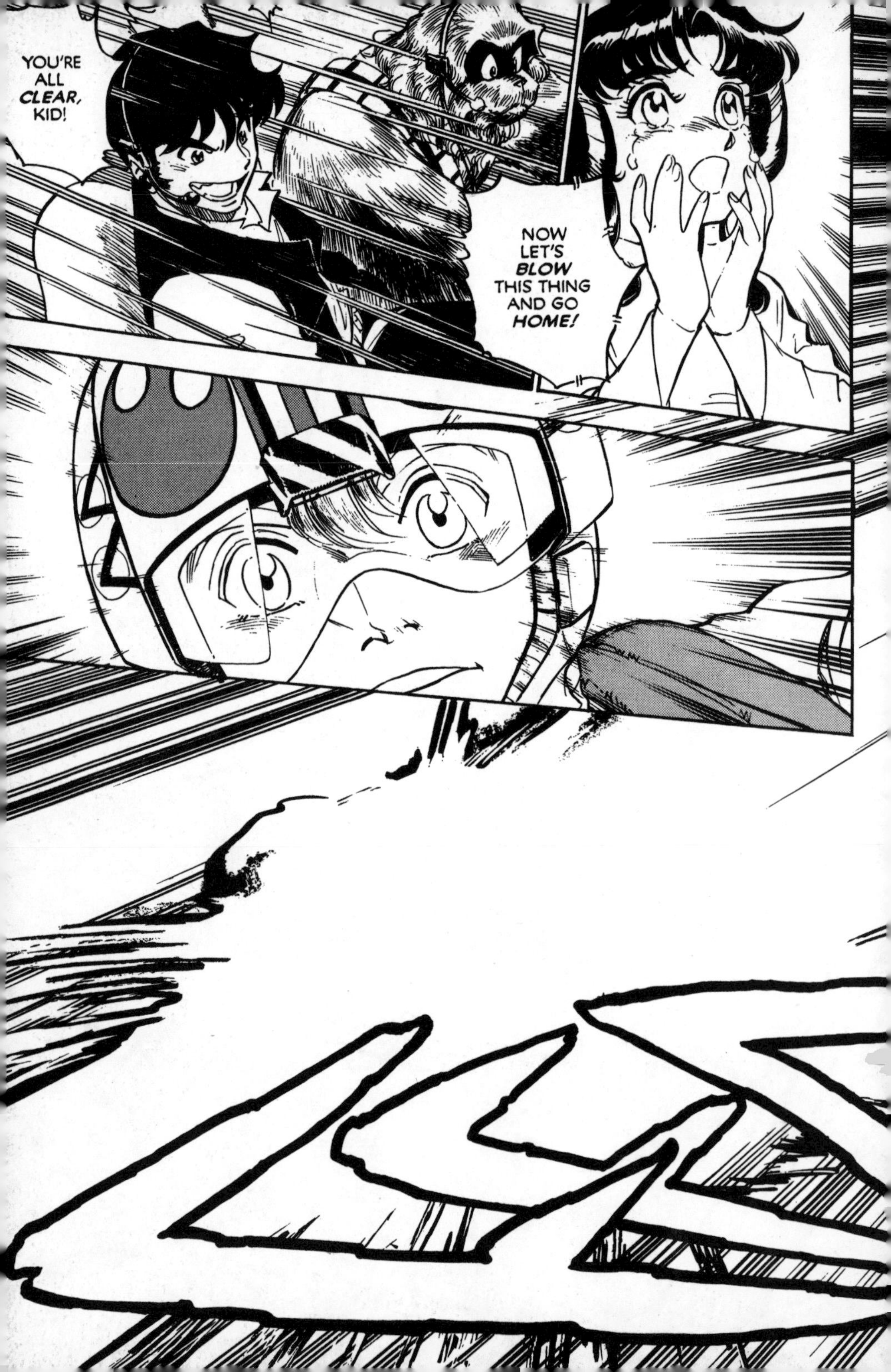
YOU'RE ALL CLEAR, KID!
NOW LET'S BLOW THIS THING AND GO HOME!

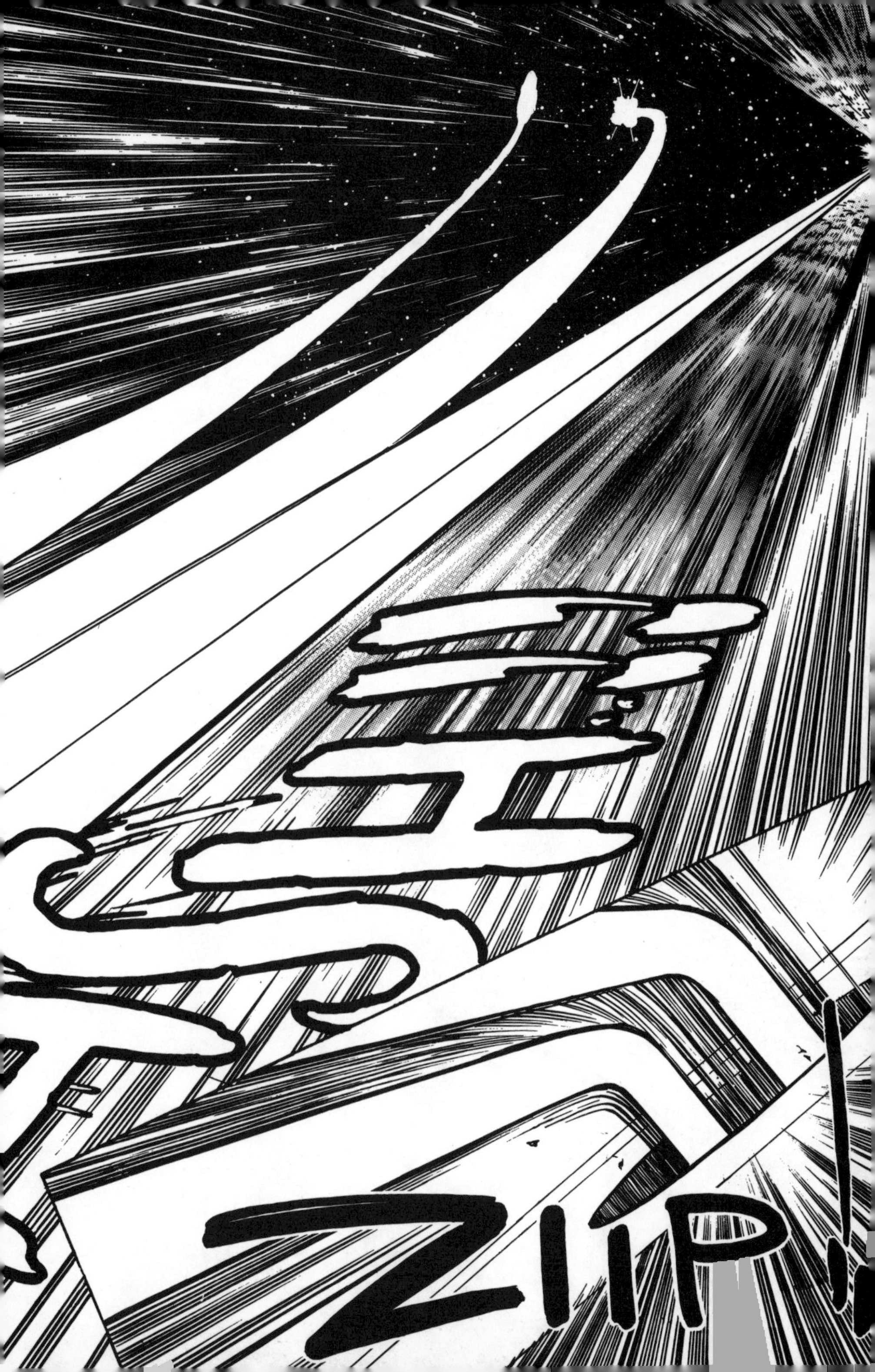
ZIIP!!

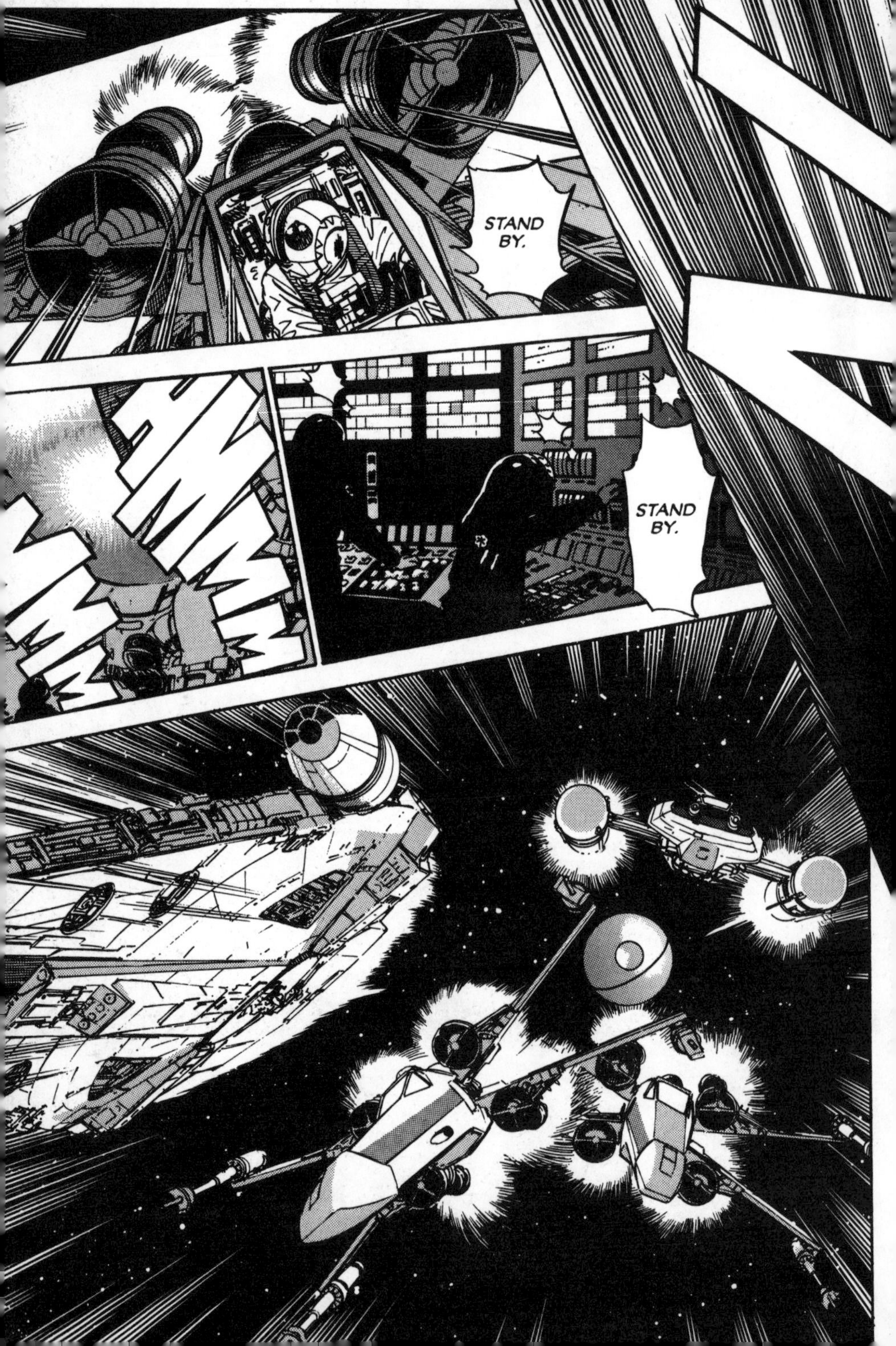
STAND BY.
STAND BY.

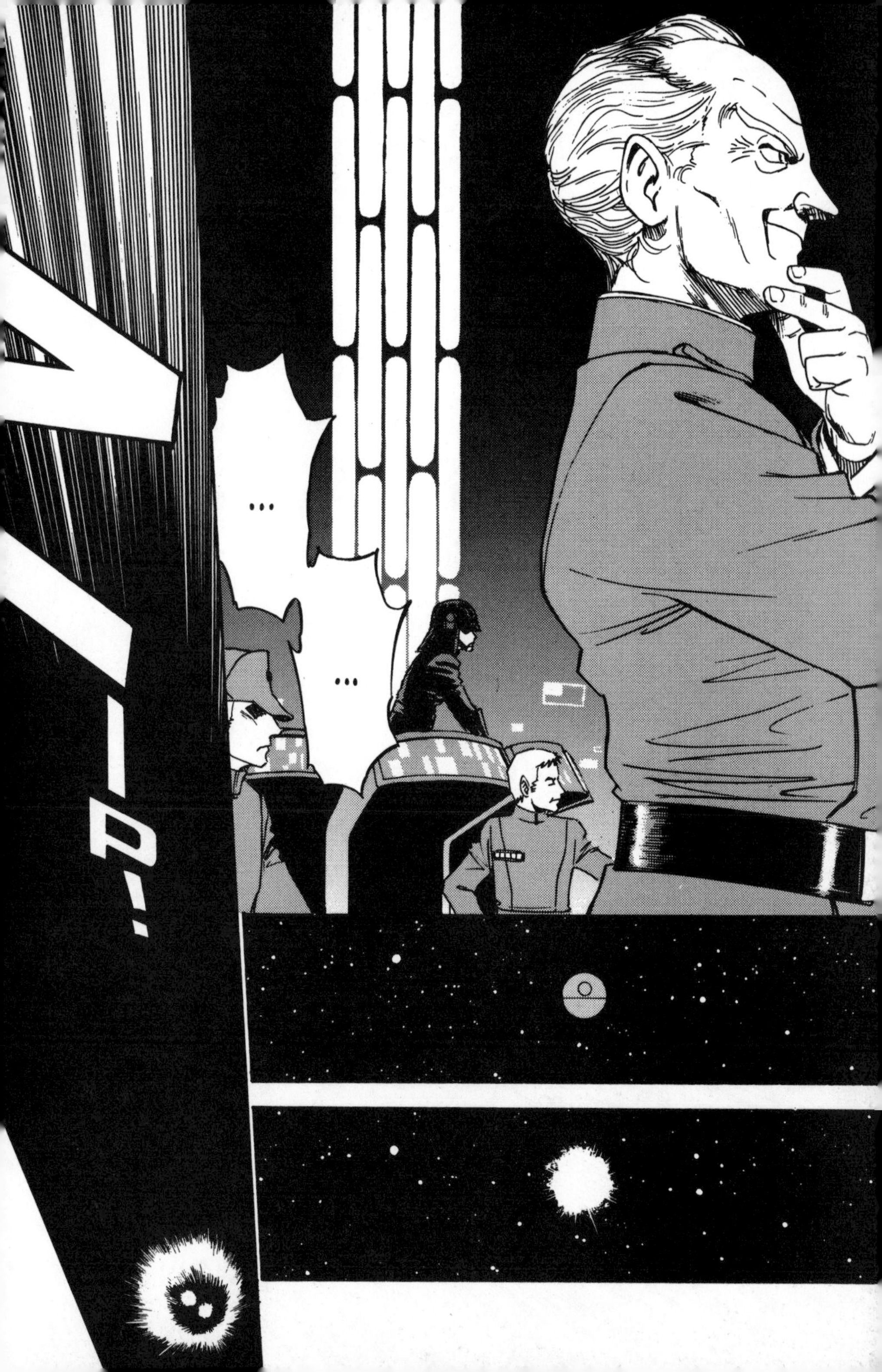
...
...

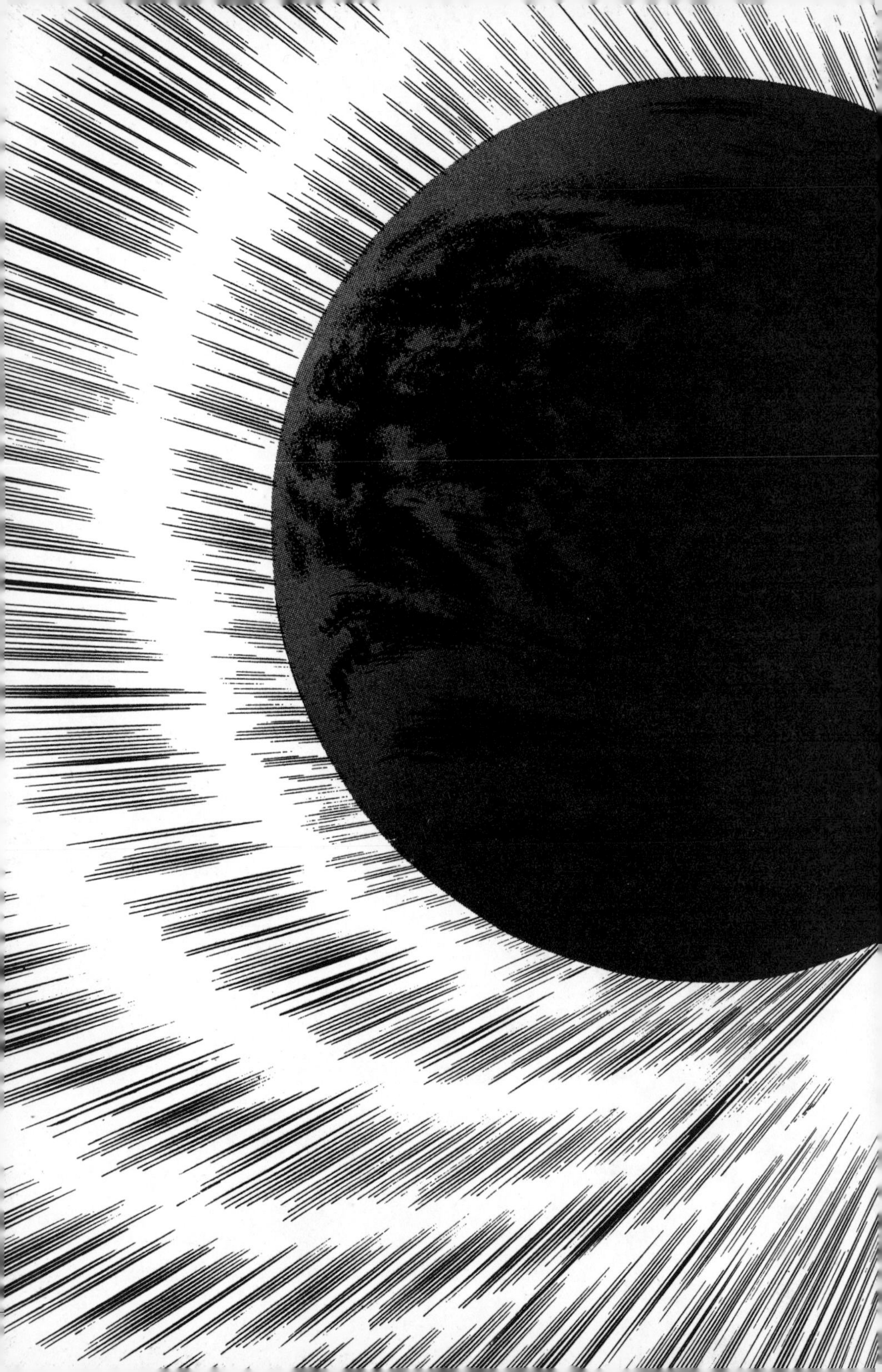

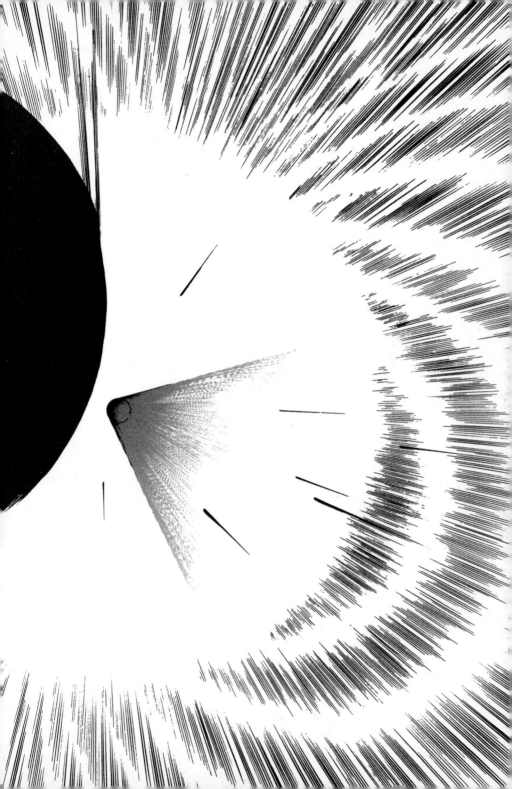

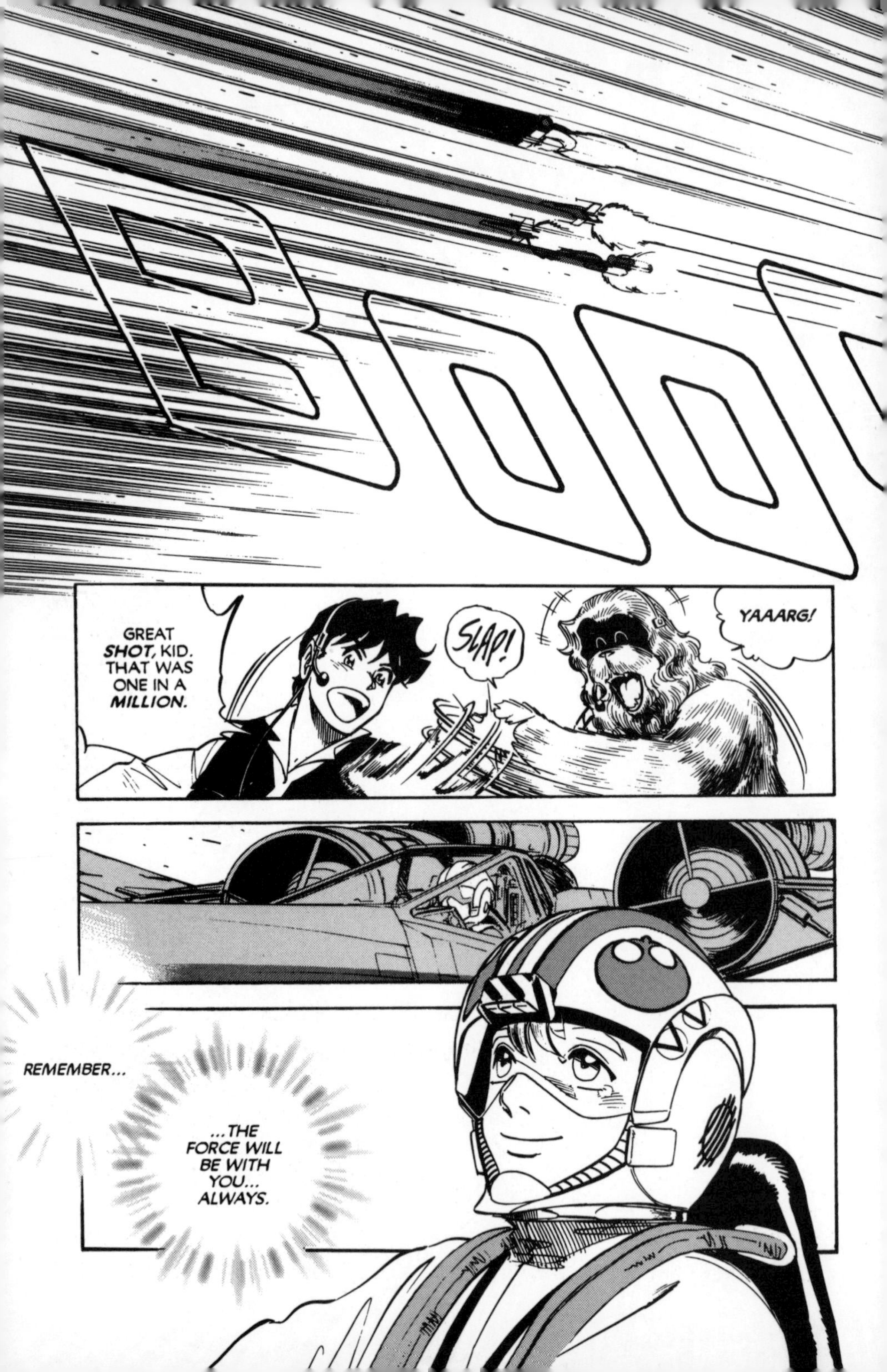
BOOO
GREAT SHOT, KID. THAT WAS ONE IN A MILLION.
SLAP!
YAAARG!
REMEMBER...
...THE FORCE WILL BE WITH YOU... ALWAYS.

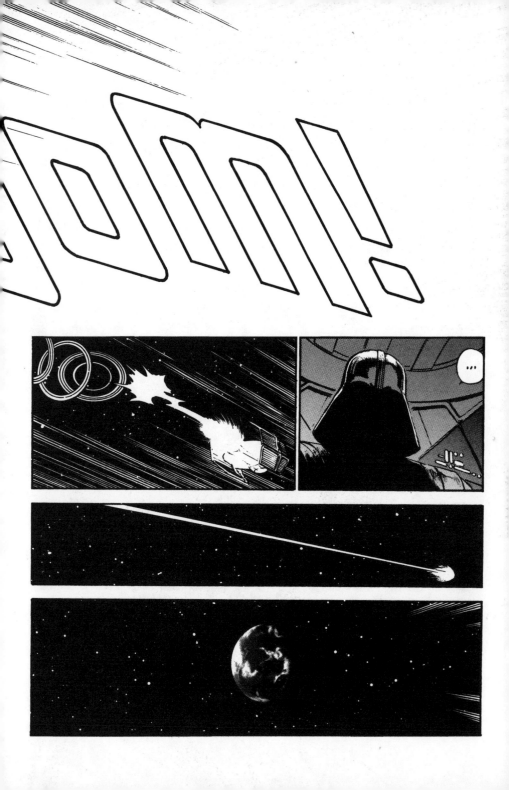

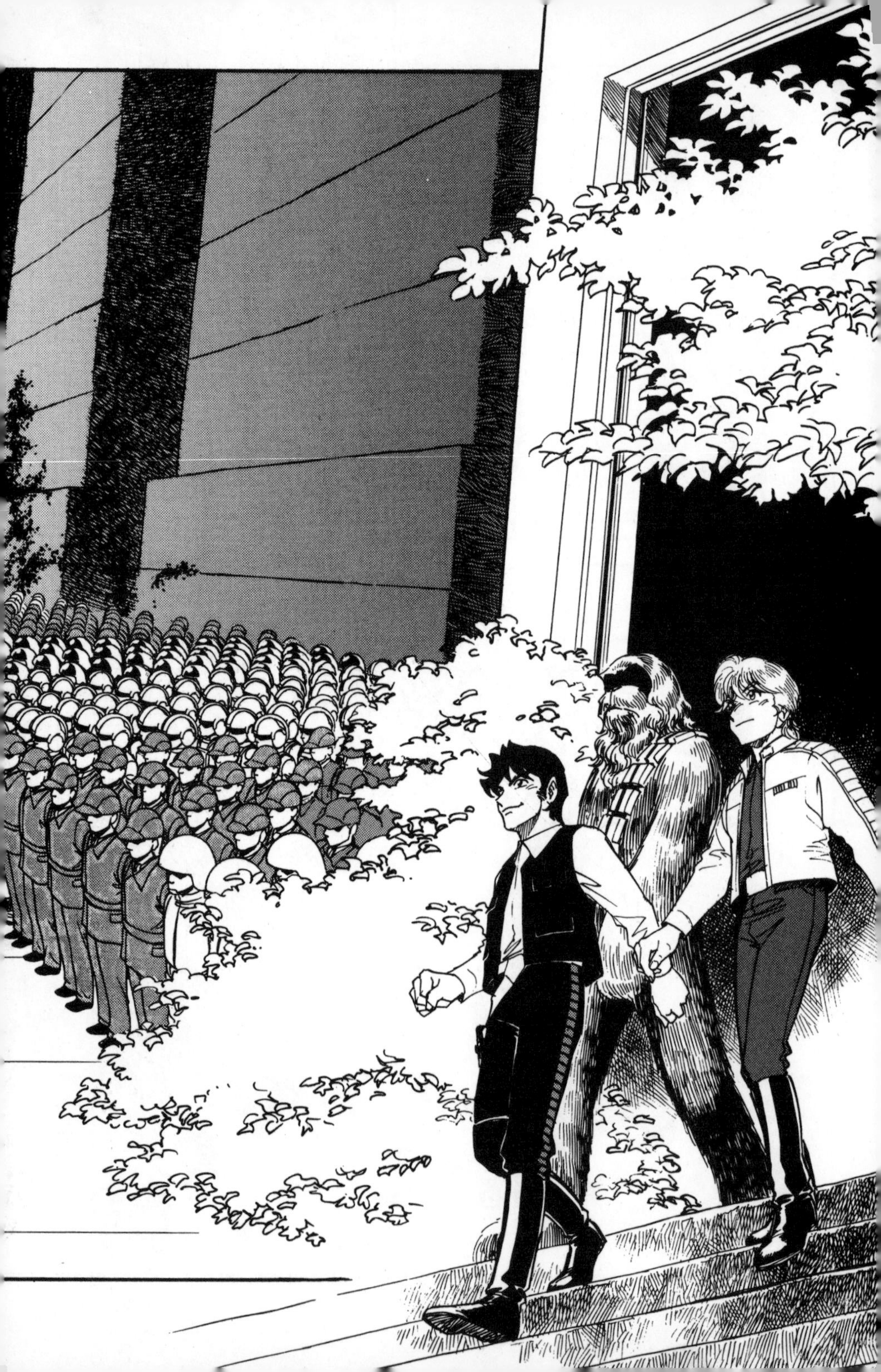

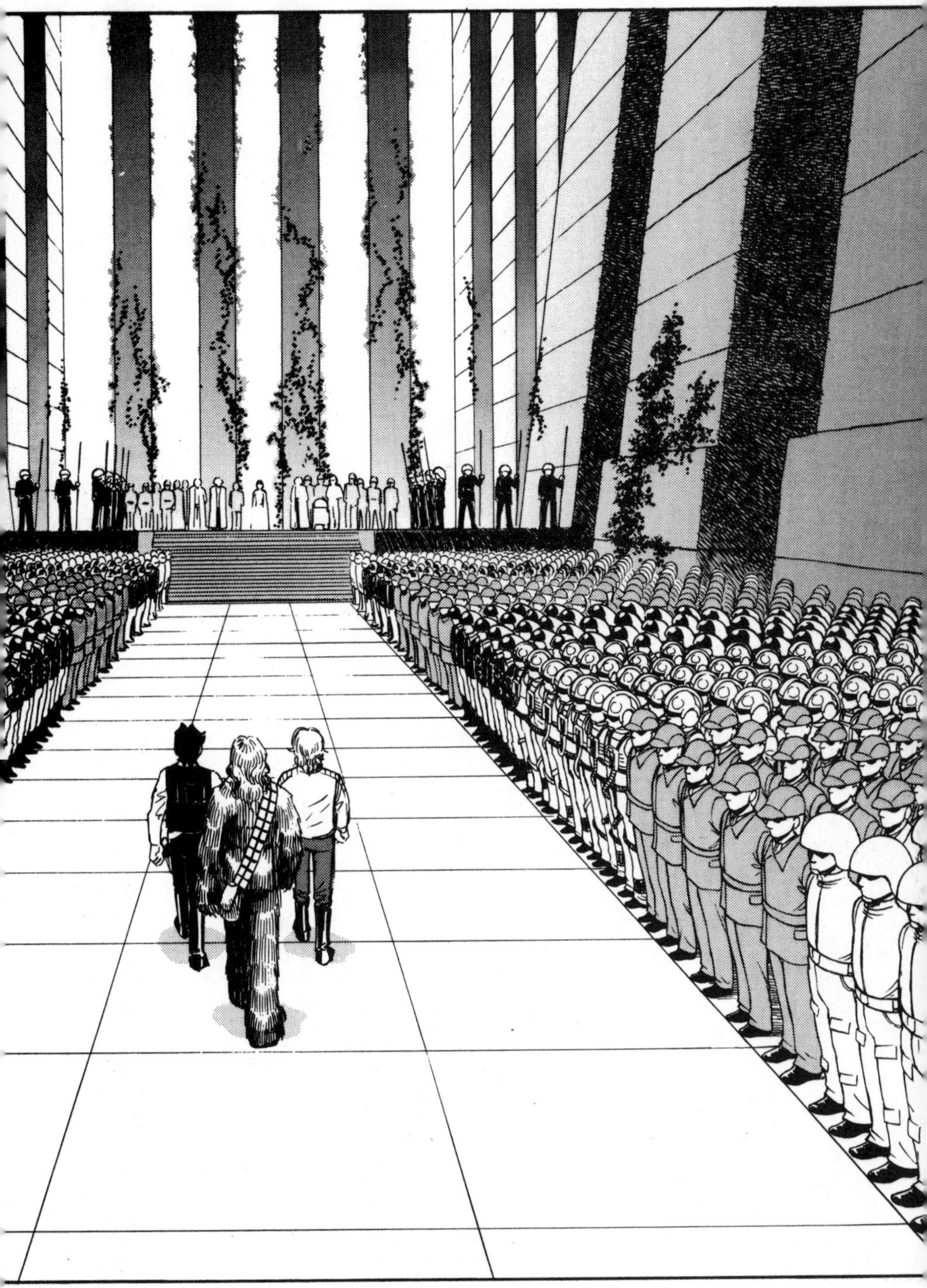

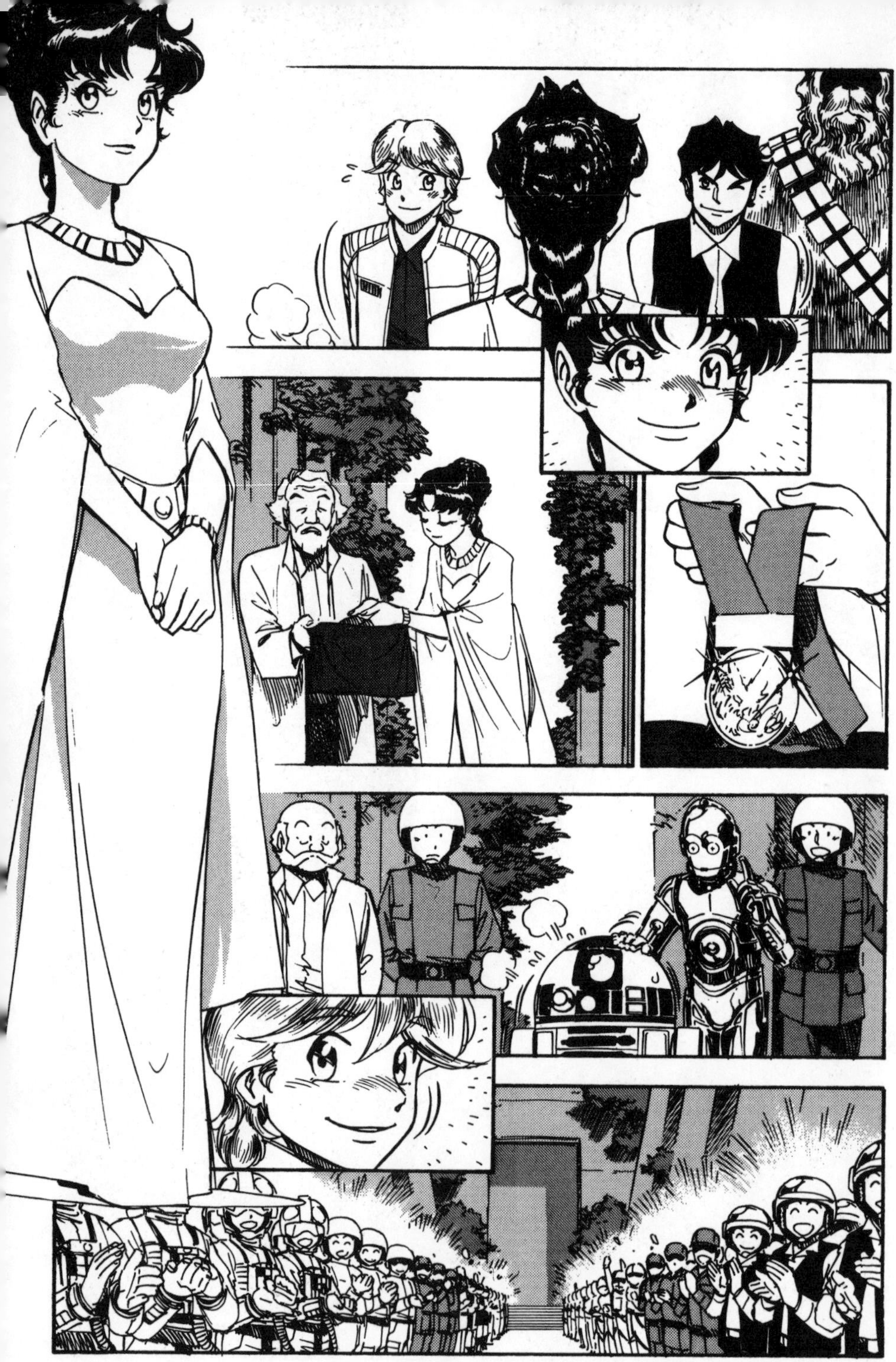

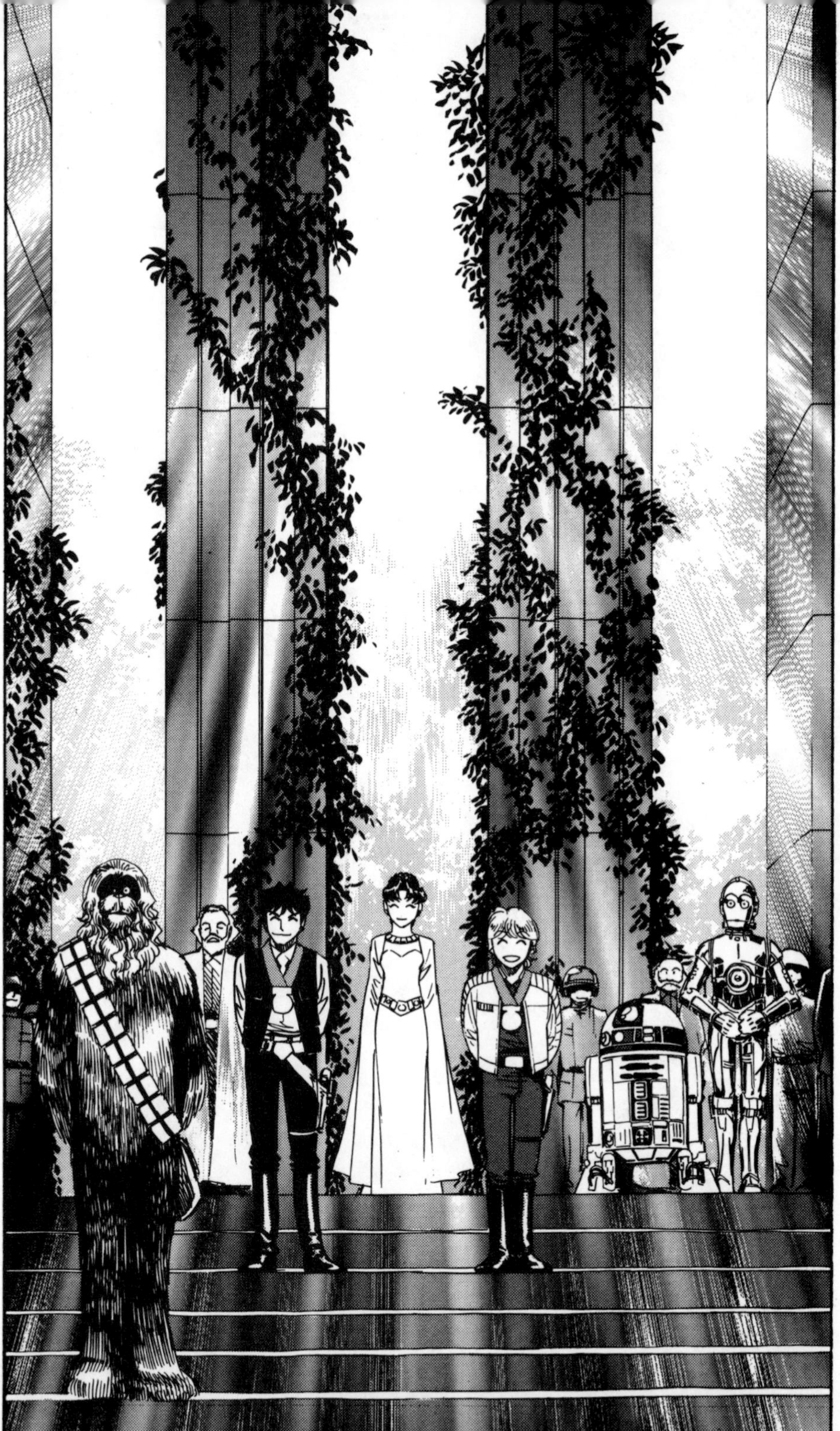

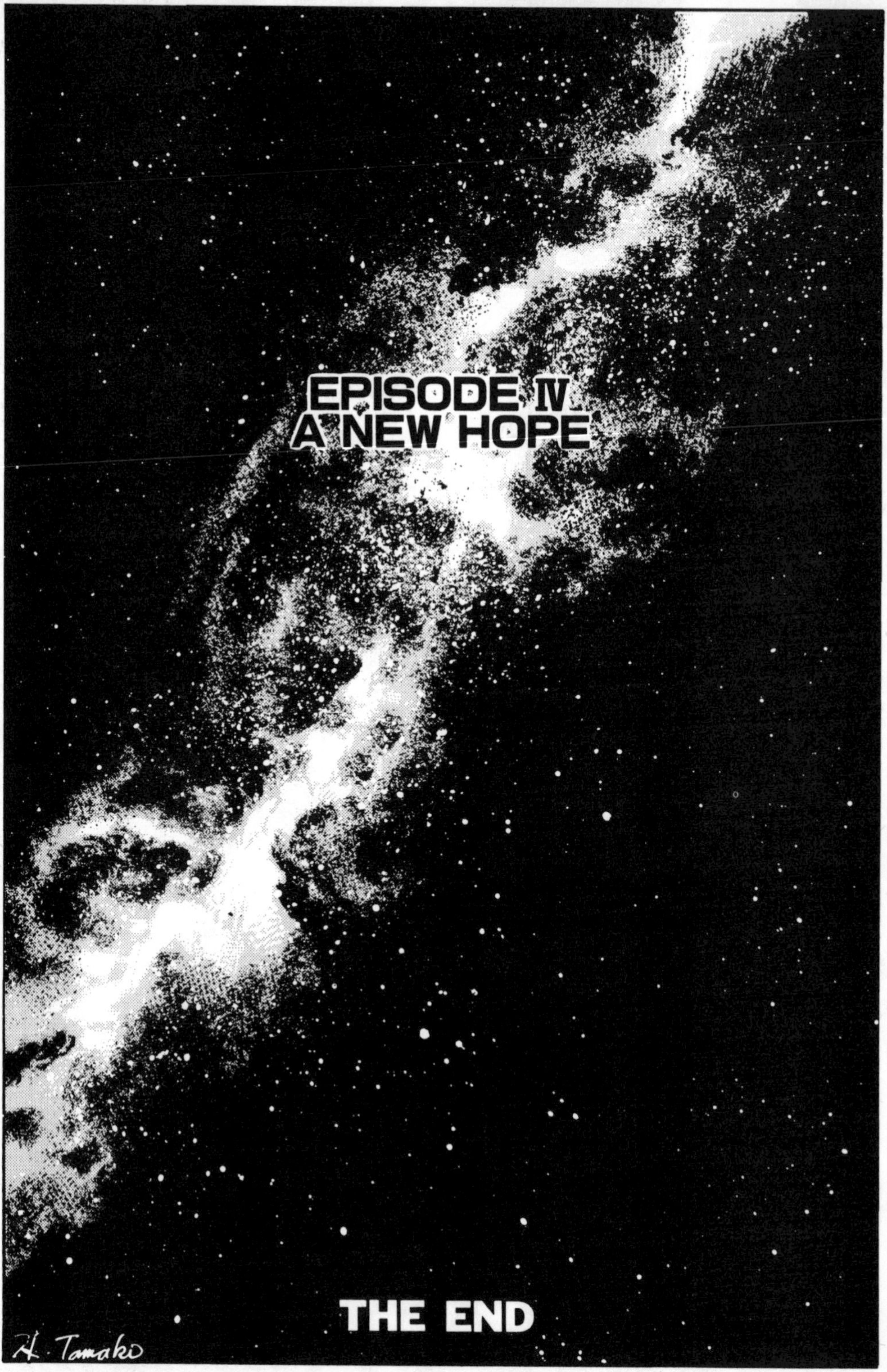
EPISODE IV
A NEW HOPE
THE END
H. Tamaki

スター・ウォーズ
HISAO TAMAKI
SKETCH GALLERY

The following is a sketch by artist Hisao Tamaki, done in preparation for his work on STAR WARS: A NEW HOPE — MANGA.

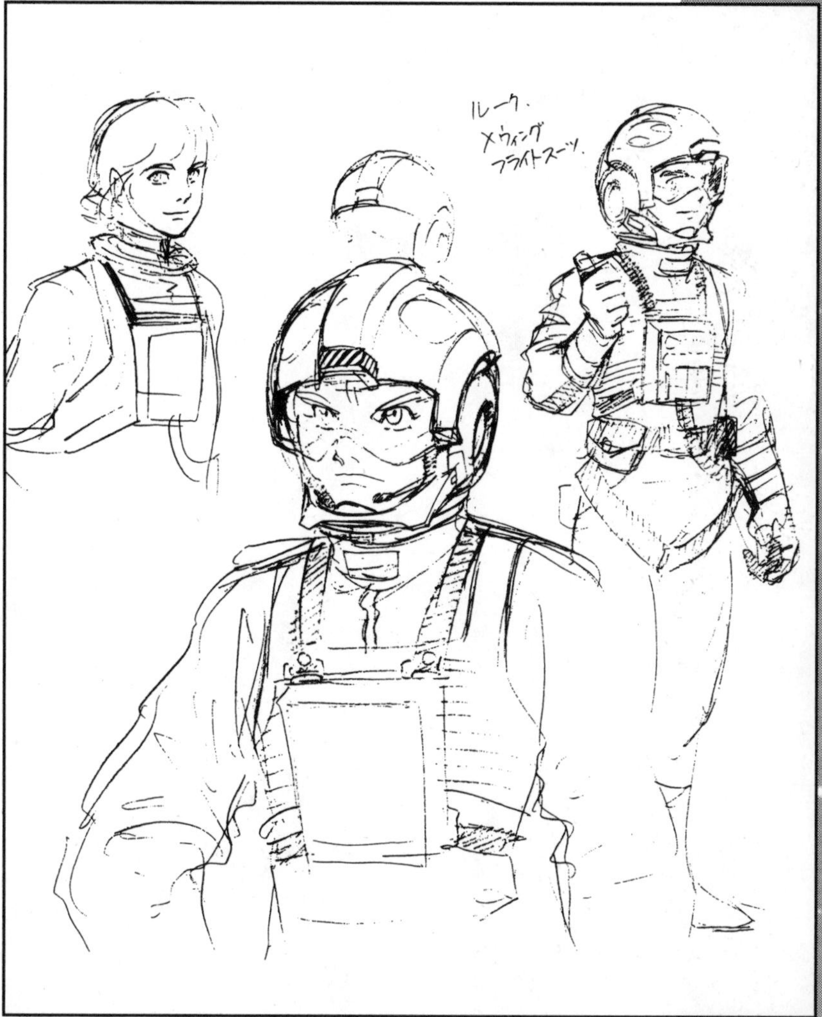
ルーク
Xウィング
フライトスーツ

LUKE SKYWALKER
IN X-WING PILOT GEAR

スター・ウォーズ
ADAM WARREN
SKETCH GALLERY

The following is a sketch by cover artist Adam Warren, done in preparation for the final cover of STAR WARS: A NEW HOPE — MANGA volume four.

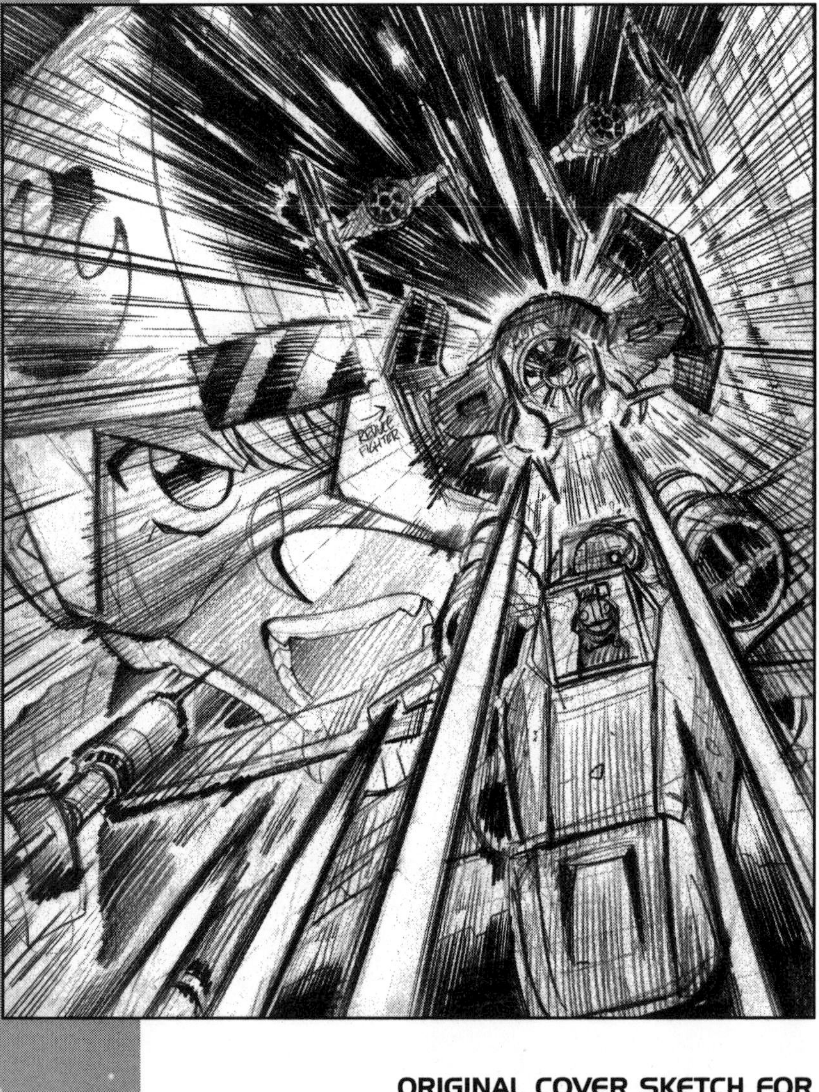
REDUCE FIGHTER

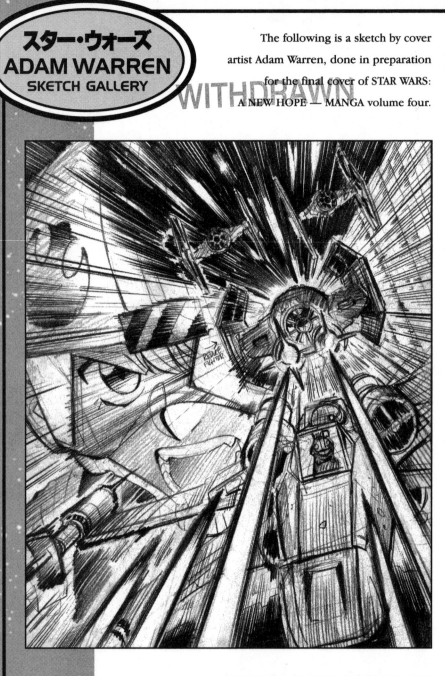

ORIGINAL COVER SKETCH FOR
STAR WARS MANGA VOLUME FOUR

ADAPTED FROM AN ORIGINAL SCRIPT BY GEORGE LUCAS

ILLUSTRATION BY HISAO TAMAKI

スター・ウォーズ ③
新たなる希望

LETTERING AND ART RETOUCH BY TOM ORZECHOWSKI

COVER ART BY ADAM WARREN

COVER COLORS BY JOSEPH WIGHT

SPECIAL THANKS TO ALLAN KAUSCH AND LUCY AUTREY WILSON AT LUCAS LICENSING

SPECIAL THANKS TO AMADOR CISNEROS AND MICHELLE STEWART

BOOK DESIGN BY CARY GRAZZINI

EDITED BY DAVID LAND

PUBLISHED BY MIKE RICHARDSON

Published by Dark Horse Comics, Inc., 10956 SE Main Street, Milwaukie, OR 97222

ISBN: 1-56971-364-2   First edition: September 1998

10 9 8 7 6 5 4 3 2

PRINTED IN THE UNITED STATES OF AMERICA

スター・ウォーズ BACKLIST

A SAMPLING OF スター・ウォーズ GRAPHIC NOVELS FROM DARK HORSE COMICS

IN DEADLY PURSUIT
ISBN: 1-56971-109-7 $16.95

THE REBEL STORM
ISBN: 1-56971-106-2 $16.95

ESCAPE TO HOTH
ISBN: 1-56971-093-7 $16.95

THE EARLY ADVENTURES
ISBN: 1-56971-178-X $19.95

HAN SOLO AT STARS' END
ISBN: 1-56971-254-9 $6.95

A NEW HOPE
ISBN: 1-56971-213-1 $9.95

THE EMPIRE STRIKES BACK
ISBN: 1-56971-234-4 $9.95

RETURN OF THE JEDI
ISBN: 1-56971-235-2 $9.95

DARK EMPIRE
ISBN: 1-56971-073-2 $17.95

DARK EMPIRE II
ISBN: 1-56971-119-4 $17.95

EMPIRE'S END
ISBN: 1-56971-306-5 $5.95

DEATH, LIES, & TREACHERY
ISBN: 1-56971-311-1 $12.95

SOLDIER FOR THE EMPIRE HC
ISBN: 1-56971-155-0 $24.95

REBEL AGENT HC
ISBN: 1-56971-156-9 $24.95

JEDI KNIGHT HC
1-56971-157-7 $24.95

SOLDIER FOR THE EMPIRE
1-56971-348-0 $14.95

DOMINION
ISBN: 1-56971-160-7 $14.95

CONFLICT 1: NO MORE NOISE
ISBN: 1-56971-233-6 $14.95

A CHILD'S DREAM
ISBN: 1-56971-140-2 $17.95

RISE OF THE DRAGON PRINCESS
ISBN: 1-56971-302-2 $12.95

GHOST IN THE SHELL
ISBN: 1-56971-081-3 $24.95

GODZILLA
ISBN: 1-56971-063-5 $17.95

AGE OF MONSTERS
ISBN: 1-56971-277-8 $17.95

PAST, PRESENT, AND FUTURE
ISBN: 1-56971-278-6 $17.95

BONNIE & CLYDE
ISBN: 1-56971-215-8 $13.95

MISFIRE
ISBN: 1-56971-253-0 $12.95

RETURN OF GRAY
ISBN: 1-56971-299-9 $17.95

ORION
ISBN: 1-56971-148-8 $17.95

1-555-GODDESS
ISBN: 1-56971-207-7 $13.95

LOVE POTION NO. 9
ISBN: 1-56971-252-2 $12.95

SYMPATHY FOR THE DEVIL
ISBN: 1-56971-329-4 $12.95

VOLUME 1
ISBN: 1-56971-161-5 $13.95

3 1901 05327 8935